Talk! Talk! Talk!

Tools to Facilitate Language

Nicole Muir, Kathryn Gerylo

Monica Gompf, Theresa Burke

Pat Lumsden, Sandra McCaig

Super Duper® Publications • Greenville, SC

06   05   04   03   07   06   05   04   03

Library of Congress Cataloging-in-Publication Data

Talk! Talk! Talk! : tools to facilitate language / Nicole Muir ... (et al.).
    p. cm.
    Includes bibliographical references.
    ISBN 1–888222–54–9
    1. Interpersonal communication in children. 2. Child rearing. I. Muir, Nicole, date.

BF723.C57 T35 2000
618.92'85506—dc21

                                                                    00–044305
                                                                    CIP

Cover Design by Debbie Olson

Printed in the United States of America

P.O. Box 24997 • Greenville, SC 29616-2497 USA
www.superduperinc.com
1-800-277-8737 • Fax 1-800-978-7379

To our own children, who introduced us to the wonder of childspeak.

To our clients—children and parents—who showed us that the journey through the world of words is intriguing, enchanting, and baffling.

To our colleagues, whose faith and encouragement provided the motivation and momentum for this project.

To those of you who read this book— may it help you continue to unravel the mystery of what makes us talk.

Contents

Preface

"What is this?" said the Unicorn upon meeting Alice lost in the woods.

"This is a child!" Haigha replied eagerly. "It's as large as life and twice as natural!"

"I always thought they were fabulous monsters," said the Unicorn. "Is it alive?"

"It can talk," said Haigha solemnly.

The Unicorn looked dreamily at Alice and said, "Talk child."

—Lewis Carroll, *Through the Looking Glass*

What the Unicorn didn't realize is that not all children talk on command. In order to speak, children need to have something to talk about, someone to talk with, and a way of saying something. They need to learn words for the things they see, do, want, and think about.

Adults must model these words for children by frequently using new vocabulary in a variety of settings. Children are never too young to be exposed to words. Babies need to develop an internal language by hearing words long before they speak them. Children must understand words before they can use them meaningfully.

Through interactive experiences, children learn to understand their world and acquire words for objects and events. As children hear and then use these words, their growing language skills allow them to discover and express the "who," "what," "when," "where," "why," and "hows" of the world. Adults, particularly caregivers, must help the children in their lives develop speech and language skills.

As speech-language pathologists working in a variety of settings with diverse populations, we have noticed that children become more competent language users when adults in their lives are effective language facilitators. Parents and educators who use language facilitation strategies report increased success in their verbal interactions with children. Language facilitation strategies have proven to be successful in encouraging children who are reluctant communicators to use language, in improving the language of children with speech and language disorders, in developing strong speech and language skills in all children, and in improving the intelligibility of children with phonological disorders.

This product was initially used by speech-language pathologists at the Child Guidance Clinic of Winnipeg, in Manitoba, Canada. The original book (entitled *We Have Ways of Making Them Talk)* has been used extensively over the past 20 years in 11 school divisions in the greater Winnipeg area, throughout the province of Manitoba, as well as in other provinces in Canada. Throughout the years, speech-language pathologists using the resource have given the book to anyone in a position to facilitate children's language development. The material was especially useful when providing workshops for parents, teachers, special education teachers, and volunteers. The original material was revised twice and printed in both English and French. These books are now out of print, however the material has been updated and revised into this newest edition: *Talk! Talk! Talk! Tools to Facilitate Language.*

Talk! Talk! Talk! evolved from our many years of experience in working with children and families. The described strategies that facilitate interactions have gained recognition because of their effectiveness when communicating with children who experience a delay in their language acquisition. Publishing *Talk! Talk! Talk!* started with an idea to put our practices into a form that others could use. We would like to acknowledge the assistance we received from Pam Diebner, Marci Krier, Jennifer Larsen, Vicki Larson, and Kristine Lofland, who reviewed the manuscript in its earlier form. Their critiques and suggestions have helped us create an easily readable publication that will provide caregivers with tools to nurture children's language development.

Kathryn, Monica, Theresa, Pat, and Sandra would also like to extend special thanks to Nicole, whose vision, energy, persistence, and technical wizardry kept us all moving toward what often seemed an elusive goal.

Introduction

Overview

Talk! Talk! Talk! Tools to Facilitate Language is a resource to help parents, caregivers, and para-professionals (i.e., adults) develop 25 listening and talking strategies to promote children's speech and language development. The strategies are known as Listening and Talking Tools and are useful for increasing vocabulary, developing sentence structure, encouraging the retelling of experiences, increasing speech intelligibility, and improving conversational interactions. Adults learn and practice the strategies through several activities. Most of the pages in *Talk! Talk! Talk!* are reproducible handouts of strategy guides and activity descriptions. The handouts are intended to provide speech-language pathologists and early childhood specialists with easy-to-access materials to use in presentations and workshops for parents and other educators.

Part I of this resource includes four chapters. The 25 Listening and Talking Tools outlined in Chapter 1 are presented individually to encourage better learning and integration by significant adults in children's lives. Summary pages, which present four or five tools per page, serve as reminders of the tools being developed and are useful as handouts. Chapters 2, 3, and 4 each focus on a specific activity—Scrapbooks, Stories, or Television and Videos. Families can participate in valuable talking and listening practice while engaged in making scrapbooks; reading, telling, and writing stories; and watching television shows or videos. These chapters show how each type of activity can be used to enhance the development of speech and language skills.

Part II includes 36 Plan-Do-Review activities to practice the Listening and Talking Tools and to promote communication in natural contexts. All the activities in Part II require little preparation on the part of the adult facilitator.

Talk! Talk! Talk! also includes three useful appendices. Appendix A provides an optional *Listening and Talking Tools Report Card* for use with adults; Appendix B contains a *Review Page* for adult learners to use with children upon completion of any activity; and Appendix C provides 12 calendars filled with daily activities to spark learning and conversation between children and caregivers.

Goals

Talk! Talk! Talk! should be used to encourage adults to acquire and use specific language facilitation strategies to help children—especially those with delayed or disordered language development—become better communicators. For children to become effective communicators, it is important that adults in their environment interact in such a way as to (1) increase children's language learning experiences and (2) maximize the effectiveness of communication exchanges. *Talk! Talk! Talk!* helps adults accomplish both of these goals. In addition, *Talk! Talk! Talk!* helps children:

- Increase language comprehension during interactions with adults

- Improve language production competencies during daily routines and while engaged in special activities

- Develop emerging literacy skills through heightened exposure to books and story structure

Target Audience

Talk! Talk! Talk! was compiled for professionals who are teaching adults how to become better language facilitators. Professionals who can successfully teach the Listening and Talking Tools presented in this book include speech-language pathologists, early childhood specialists, guidance counselors, and social workers. Adults who should learn the Listening and Talking Tools include parents, caregivers, teaching assistants, paraprofessionals, volunteers, and anyone else who enjoys communicating with young children.

The Listening and Talking Tools presented are universal and, if translated, can be used by adults speaking any language. The tools are also appropriate for use in any setting in both rural and urban areas: home, school, daycare, special-education classes, hospitals, clinics, and early childhood programs. *Talk! Talk! Talk!* is an excellent resource for adults working with children who have delayed or disordered language, as well as children who are developing language normally.

Rationale
Early Language Experiences

Talk! Talk! Talk! is a powerful tool to use with all families, but it can be especially helpful for economically disadvantaged families given that the language input experiences of children from those families are enormously different (Hart and Risley, 1995). As a comparison, Hart and Risley reported that children in welfare* families hear an average of 620 words per hour; children in working-class* families hear approximately 1,250 words per hour; and children in professional* families hear about 2,150 words per hour. Extrapolating from these data, by age 3, children in welfare families have had 10 million fewer words of cumulative language experience than children in working-class families and 20 million fewer words than children in professional families (Hart and Risley). When children are so linguistically delayed at an early age, it is difficult for them to catch up.

The linguistic exposure children receive prior to age 3 has an enormous effect on their speech and language abilities and cognitive skills when measured at age 3 and again at age 9

*The terms *welfare, working-class,* and *professional* are the researchers' reported terms; the authors recommend not using these terms with families.

(Hart and Risley, 1995). *Talk! Talk! Talk!* is designed to prevent the need for "catching up" (regardless of the socioeconomic status of the family) by teaching family members, as well as other significant adults, strategies to increase and improve their talking time with their children.

Caregivers as Educators

Speech-language pathologists and early childhood specialists have come to recognize the importance of helping significant adults in children's environments develop more effective interaction skills (Girolametto, 1986; Girolametto, Greenberg, and Manolson, 1986; Tannock, Girolametto, and Siegel, 1992). The role of the adult becomes that of a language facilitator, guiding and encouraging children to become active participants in language exchanges, to develop turn-taking skills, and to acquire new language forms and structures. Children naturally learn language by hearing others around them talk about activities and daily events. For example, a child is taking part in a language experience when an adult describes the things they see together during a car ride.

Adults need to be effective language facilitators when communicating with young children, especially when conversing with children who present language learning difficulties. When children's language skills are delayed or disordered, adults may not know what they can do differently, especially if they either have a child or have taught other children who developed appropriate language abilities with seemingly no special effort. These adults may be confused and may struggle to find strategies to help those children develop appropriate language skills. Adults often require assistance recognizing and understanding children's strengths, weaknesses, and needs. By helping the significant adults in children's lives develop an awareness of communication behaviors and the use of facilitative strategies, children's speech and language skills can improve.

Talk! Talk! Talk! teaches strategies and provides activities designed to help adults improve their listening and talking skills with children, even when children can "hold the floor" during conversation. Hart and Risley (1999) found that when children began talking as much as other family members, the amount those family members talked leveled off. They also found that on average, children at 28 months talked as much as their parents "and parent utterances to the children began a steady decline in number" (p. 10). Adults must keep talking to children, using new words and word combinations, to provide the level of language experience children need to continue to progress.

Selection of Strategies

Language facilitation strategies are frequently described in the literature as an effective way to assist children with language disorders in becoming better communicators (Bruner, 1978; Cole, 1995; Muma, 1971; Norris and Hoffman, 1990). The language facilitation strategies outlined in *Talk! Talk! Talk!* come from a variety of sources, including literature related to early language development (Brown, 1973; Bruner, 1978), studies of pragmatic skill development (Dore, 1974; Duchan, 1984), and naturalistic intervention practices (Fey, 1986; Norris and Hoffman, 1990). The use of language facilitation strategies is consistent with the tenets of naturalistic language intervention, specifically that a child learns language best in the context of real-life daily activities and interactions (Norris and Hoffman). These language facilitation strategies are also based on adults' communication behaviors that contribute most to the development of accomplished linguistic skills and heightened cognitive skills in children (Hart and Risley, 1995). Using language facilitation strategies gives adults the necessary Listening and Talking Tools to help children focus on the meaningful aspects of the environment, which allows children to function as active participants during interactions. Communication is expanded and refined within meaningful settings, thereby facilitating language development in the environment where new skills will be used (Noonan and McCormick, 1993).

As a result of using the language facilitation strategies in this resource, adults can increase both the quantity and quality of their verbal interactions with children, and children will consequently improve their listening and speaking skills, which will ultimately help develop their reading and writing skills. Emerging literacy is highly influenced by adults as they expose children to books and help them develop vocabulary knowledge well before a child begins formal schooling (Butler, 1999).

Some authors argue that language intervention programs should include both direct contact with the child and adult participation so that the adults can learn appropriate intervention techniques (Fey and Cleave, 1997; Fey, Cleave, Long, and Hughes, 1993). The challenge for professionals is to find an effective means of teaching new behaviors to adults so that these strategies can become an integral part of their daily interactions with children.

Training programs for adults, such as the Hanen program, have become an important feature in both prevention and intervention language models (Watson, 1993). *Talk! Talk! Talk!* was not developed to replace existing training programs. Rather, it was designed to be an additional resource to facilitate new communication skills in adults and to help them implement these skills during their daily interactions with children. It is also a helpful resource for adults who are unable to attend or who do not feel comfortable in formal training programs.

Contents of *Talk! Talk! Talk!*
Getting Started with the Listening and Talking Tools
Chapter 1 presents 25 Listening and Talking Tools that can be used by adults to encourage the development of language in children. These language facilitation strategies are valuable for all age levels and improve the communication skills of both adults and children. The

strategies are described in a user-friendly, easy-to-remember pictorial format geared to reach a wide audience.

The Listening and Talking Tools are first presented individually on reproducible pages to encourage learning and integration of the strategies into the adult's repertoire. After every four or five strategies, there is a reproducible summary page designed to help adults learn and remember the facilitation strategies. Opportunities and suggestions for helping adults practice these strategies are provided in Chapters 2, 3, and 4; in Part II; and in the appendices.

Scrapbooks

Chapter 2 provides background information, strategy guides, and activity handouts so that adults can better understand how to create and use scrapbooks with children. Creating scrapbooks with children provides additional opportunities for adults to practice language facilitation strategies. In addition, the scrapbook pages can be used to teach children new vocabulary, to develop classification and categorization skills in children, and to promote children's storytelling skills.

During scrapbook activities, adults can practice the Listening and Talking Tools taught in Chapter 1. Adults and children can put a variety of items into scrapbooks, including photographs, illustrations, and souvenirs. Adults should transcribe a child's ideas or stories to go with the included items. These written records help other adults share past events with children. When children are sharing information with an unfamiliar listener, a scrapbook provides the listener with important knowledge of what took place, thereby allowing them to provide the necessary scaffolding for children who may have difficulty expressing ideas verbally.

Stories

Story reading, storytelling, and story writing are the focus of Chapter 3. The use of Listening and Talking Tools during narrative tasks enhances the quality of the activities so that heightened speech, language, and literacy skills may result.

In Chapter 3, adults learn the importance of narrative activities and how to incorporate language facilitation strategies into story-reading, storytelling, and story-writing tasks. Suggestions are also provided regarding how to read with children, how to select appropriate books, and how to help children "write" their own stories. Professionals are encouraged to help adults incorporate daily reading times into children's schedules and to utilize local resources, such as bookstores and libraries.

Television and Videos

Adults can make television and video watching a more interactive, language learning activity by using language facilitation strategies. Background information and strategy guides are provided in Chapter 4 to help adults understand how to promote language learning and communication while children are watching their favorite television shows or videos. Adult questions and comments can help children develop an understanding of how stories develop and the concepts that are within a story. During television and video activities, adults can encourage children to talk about past and possible future events in the stories.

It is not being suggested that language skills can be developed exclusively through the medium of television or videos. However, this chapter has been included because television shows and videos are often a major influence in children's lives. The challenge is to turn passive viewing into active language learning by asking and answering questions about the stories and characters.

Plan-Do-Review Activities

The Plan-Do-Review activities in Part II provide opportunities to practice the Listening and Talking Tools introduced in Chapter 1. These activities encourage conversations and provide a reason for adults and children to talk and listen to each other. The 36 Plan-Do-Review activities are organized based on common early education classroom themes (e.g., *Seasons* and *Transportation*). The activities are fun, easy, and can be included as part of a typical day at home or at school. Minimal preparation is required for the activities, and any required materials can be located with ease, either in this book or around the home or classroom.

Suggestions for using the Plan-Do-Review activities are summarized at the beginning of Part II (see page 83). Two introductory pages are also provided (see pages 84–85) to help adults become familiar with the concept of Plan-Do-Review activities and the three steps involved. A *Plan-Do-Review Activity Worksheet* is provided and can be used by adults when they are preparing an assigned Plan-Do-Review activity (see page 86). This worksheet can also be used by adults when they are creating their own Plan-Do-Review activities to conduct with children.

Appendices
Listening and Talking Tools Report Card

Appendix A includes a generic *Listening and Talking Tools Report Card* that adults can use to monitor their own use of the Listening and Talking Tools during their daily interactions with children.

Review Page

A *Review Page* is included in Appendix B as a guide for adults and children to use when talking about completed activities. Talking through a *Review Page* with a child provides the adult with yet another opportunity to use language facilitation strategies with a child. In addition, adults can use completed *Review Pages* to reflect on their own use of Listening and Talking Tools and children's communication skills during activities. Review pages can be used by adults and children following the completion of any sort of activity (e.g., finishing a Plan-Do-Review activity, completing a scrapbook page, watching a television show, reading a story, creating a craft activity).

Calendars

The 12 calendars in Appendix C provide suggestions for simple daily activities that encourage communicative interactions between young children and adults. These calendars are best suited for use in home settings, as many of the activities require materials from around the house. The calendars provide additional opportunities for adults, specifically parents, to practice their Listening and Talking Tools. Appendix C also includes an introductory page for educators, as well as one for the adult learners.

Using *Talk! Talk! Talk!*

When professionals such as speech-language pathologists, early childhood educators, or other educators use *Talk! Talk! Talk!,* they must first identify the target audience that will be learning the language facilitation strategies. Typically the audience will be parents and/or other caregivers in the child's home setting or paraprofessionals and/or assistants in school settings.

Note that *Talk! Talk! Talk!* can also be a valuable resource for preschool teachers, early childhood teachers, and other early educators who may need to improve their own language facilitation strategies. When working with young children who are beginning to talk, educators should use Listening and Talking Tools to expand children's language from gestures and eye-gazes to the development of first words, from single words into sentences, and from sentences into conversations. The authors have made the assumption that educators who would use *Talk! Talk! Talk!* are already skilled in using Listening and Talking Tools and are equipped to teach others.

Language facilitation strategies can be taught during home visits, through small-group activities, or during one-on-one sessions in school or clinic settings depending on the logistics of space, time, and individual need. Whatever the delivery model, the first priority is to have the adult learners acquire the 25 Listening and Talking Tools delineated in Chapter 1.

Starting Out

During the first session with the adult learners, provide one of the two handouts designed for them: Talk! Talk! Talk! *An Introduction for Caregivers* (page 13) or Talk! Talk! Talk! *An Introduction for Paraprofessionals* (page 14). After reviewing the handout, be prepared to present and discuss the introductory pages for the Listening and Talking Tools (pages 21 and 28–29) and at least a few of the Listening and Talking Tools (e.g., the first five Listening and Talking Tools). At subsequent sessions, introduce other print material supplied in *Talk! Talk! Talk!* (e.g., another set of Listening and Talking Tools, Chapter 2, or Chapter 3) at a pace that is comfortable to participants and that permits the adult learners to successfully apply the tools they are learning. Be sure to help the adult learners memorize and practice at least one set of Listening and Talking Tools before introducing the supplemental information provided in Chapters 2, 3, and 4 and before introducing and assigning any Plan-Do-Review activities from Part II.

Choosing an Instructional Technique

Determine a method for introducing and practicing the strategies and for explaining the activities. Some options include:

- Model the tool with an actual child, either "live" before the participants or on video-tape. The modeling could show a participant from a previous training group or the professional in a taped sample.

- Coach the adults as they practice a new strategy while interacting with children. (Consider having the adults take turns assuming the role of the child while practicing new strategies with each other.)

- Conduct a role-play between two professionals while participants observe. Discuss the role-play and strategies that were observed.

- Conduct a role-play between one professional and one participant. After each role-play, talk about the observed behaviors.

- Lead role-plays between groups of two participants, with one adult in each group playing the role of the child.

Note that the last three choices necessitate a group setting, something not typically available during home visits. The structure of the session will determine how the Listening and Talking Tools are introduced and practiced.

Recording Interactions

Be aware that when Listening and Talking Tools are first introduced, most adults feel that they are already using these strategies with children. Upon closer observation, for example when adult-child interactions are audiotaped or videotaped and analyzed, it becomes obvious that many adults do not consistently interact in this manner with children. To this end, the use of audiotaping and videotaping is very powerful. As tools are introduced during the training sessions, arrange to have participants taped while practicing the strategies with children. If appropriate, share each individual's recording with the group and have participants encourage each other in terms of what might be changed or improved when using the Listening and Talking Tools. Encourage and model the use of constructive feedback. Arrange audiotaping or videotaping sessions whenever possible to document progress during different stages of the group or individual sessions. Encourage adults to audiotape or videotape their own interactions with their children in order to monitor their amount and style of talking.

Determining Rate of Instruction

All 25 of the Listening and Talking Tools are important for fostering understanding and use of language. It is critical that adults be given the opportunity to understand and practice each strategy before being expected to integrate several tools while interacting with children. The authors' experience has shown that adults learn the Listening and Talking Tools best when they are asked to focus on and practice one strategy at a time. Consequently, all the Listening and Talking Tools are outlined one per page to help the adult fully understand each strategy. Each page can serve as a useful overhead and handout during training programs.

Direct adults to practice each new Listening and Talking Tool during the course of a few days or a week, concentrating on the strategies taught most recently. Gradually encourage combinations of the Listening and Talking Tools until they become more and more habitual to the adult learners. The activities in *Talk! Talk! Talk!* can be used for practicing a single strategy and for practicing several strategies at once. Summary sheets, including four or five Listening and Talking Tools per page, are provided and serve as useful reminders and handouts when adult learners are ready to combine a number of strategies. The one-page Listening and Talking Tools handouts and the summary sheets can be included in parent newsletters or posted on bulletin boards to highlight certain strategies. Encourage adults to post their handouts in prominent locations to serve as reminders while they interact with children throughout the day.

Promoting Use of Strategies and Generalization

Once adults begin to combine strategies, have them use the *Listening and Talking Tools Report Card* included in Appendix A to keep track of how often they are using each strategy.

The *Listening and Talking Tools Report Card* is a useful means of evaluating when tools are being used consistently and when tools need to be used more often. Whenever an adult is audiotaped or videotaped with a child, the professional and the adult can analyze the interaction, using the *Listening and Talking Tools Report Card* to note how often the various Listening and Talking Tools are being utilized. This becomes a powerful tool for helping adults and children develop needed skills.

Educate participants on the importance of talking to children frequently and encouragingly. Remind them that even when children appear to be holding their own in conversation, it is still critical to interact often with them. Explain that children who hear only 600 words per hour will be at a severe disadvantage in their language development (Hart and Risley, 1999). Make the message to adults very clear: *Talk frequently using many different words, tell children about the world around them, and listen intently when children talk.* Challenge adults using *Talk! Talk! Talk!* to aim for 2,000+ words per hour when using the activities in this resource.

Conclusion

Talk! Talk! Talk! provides adults and children with a myriad of experiences to communicate about. Professionals may need to remind adult learners that talking with children is a joy, and that by using the Listening and Talking Tools, they can make a positive difference in children's abilities to communicate, learn, and grow.

Talk! Talk! Talk!
An Introduction for Caregivers

You are going to learn a set of Listening and Talking Tools for communicating with your child. These tools are called *language facilitation strategies* because they are designed to help your child become a better communicator. These strategies are taken from a book called *Talk! Talk! Talk!* I will also assign activities from this same book for you to do with your child.

Talking to your child is important. The Listening and Talking Tools will encourage your child to communicate more frequently and effectively. The language activities you will be assigned can help your child develop a curiosity and understanding about the world. These activities can also help your child learn and use new words.

You will learn and practice one Listening and Talking Tool at a time. Once you feel comfortable using a new strategy, we will move on to another. Ultimately, you will be comfortable using several strategies at once while you talk and play with your child.

Some Listening and Talking Tools will feel very familiar to you. You are probably already using many of the strategies. We will still spend some time focusing on each tool to make certain you are using it to its fullest advantage. Occasionally you may be audiotaped or videotaped while interacting with your child so that you can observe yourself.

You will receive a handout of each of the Listening and Talking Tools. To remind yourself to use each strategy every day, keep a copy of the handout in a prominent location (e.g., on the refrigerator door). After you have learned several strategies, you will get a summary page. The summary pages are reminders to use more than one tool at a time. You might find it easier to post the summary pages rather than the pages that show only one tool.

You will also receive a *Listening and Talking Tools Report Card.* You can use this form to record the tools you use when communicating with your child. It will help you identify the tools you need to use more frequently. The report card will be a guide when you talk with me about your strategy use and your child's development.

I look forward to helping you learn the Listening and Talking Tools!

Talk! Talk! Talk!

An Introduction for Paraprofessionals

You are going to learn a set of Listening and Talking Tools for communicating with children. These tools are called *language facilitation strategies* because they are designed to help children become better communicators. These strategies are taken from a book called *Talk! Talk! Talk!* I will also assign activities from this same book for you to do with children you work with.

The Listening and Talking Tools will encourage children to communicate more frequently and effectively. The language activities you are assigned can help children develop a curiosity and understanding about the world. These activities can also help children learn and use new words.

You will learn and practice one Listening and Talking Tool at a time. Once you feel comfortable using a new strategy, we will move on to another. Ultimately, you will be comfortable using several strategies at once while you talk and play with children.

Some Listening and Talking Tools will feel very familiar to you. You are probably already using many of the strategies. We will still spend some time focusing on each tool to make certain you are using it to its fullest advantage. Occasionally you may be audiotaped or videotaped while interacting with a child so that you can observe yourself.

You will receive a handout of each of the Listening and Talking Tools. To remind yourself to use each strategy every day, keep a copy of the handout in a prominent location (e.g., on a cabinet door). After you have learned several strategies, you will get a summary page. The summary pages are reminders to use more than one tool at a time. You might find it easier to post the summary pages rather than the pages that show only one tool.

You will also receive a *Listening and Talking Tools Report Card.* You can use this form to record the tools you use when communicating with children. It will help you identify the tools you could use more frequently. The report card will be a guide when you talk with me about your strategy use and an individual child's development.

I look forward to helping you learn the Listening and Talking Tools!

Part I

Instructional
Materials

—Instructional Materials—

The Instructional Materials included in *Talk! Talk! Talk!* consist of the following four chapters:

1. Getting Started with the Listening and Talking Tools
2. Scrapbooks
3. Stories
4. Television and Videos

Each chapter includes an informational page for the educator and an array of reproducible instructional pages for adult learners to work through.

Chapter 1 helps adults learn the 25 Listening and Talking Tools that support and encourage speech and language development in children. Each Listening and Talking Tool is presented on a full page with an example and illustration. Periodically, a summary page is provided that presents four or five Listening and Talking Tools.

Chapter 2 includes ideas that help adults apply strategies for creating and using scrapbooks with children. The Listening and Talking Tools that are taught in Chapter 1 are reinforced throughout Chapter 2.

Chapter 3 focuses on the ever important use of reading, telling, and writing stories with children. Adults learn how to use the Listening and Talking Tools along with stories to encourage speech and language development.

Chapter 4 addresses the topic of the role of electronic media in children's lives. Adults are provided with suggested guidelines to make television and video watching more meaningful for children.

It is recommended that Chapter 1 be worked through at least in part before moving on to the other chapters. Chapters 2–4 can then be used as the adult learners practice and continue to learn the Listening and Talking Tools.

The *Listening and Talking Tools Report Card* provided in Appendix A (page 130) should be distributed to adults as needed to help them monitor their own use of the strategies. The *Review Page* in Appendix B (page 131) should be provided to adults as they are assigned activities from Chapters 2–4 and from Part II. A calendar from Appendix C should be provided to adults at the beginning of each month.

Chapter 1

Getting Started with the Listening and Talking Tools

The following chapter provides reproducible pages to use when teaching the 25 Listening and Talking Tools that are designed to encourage language development in children. Ideally, all 25 strategies should be taught directly to the adult learners. It is not recommended that the reproducible pages be distributed without providing the needed guidance and practice to help adults better understand and use each strategy. Working with parents in their homes is an ideal situation; however, working with a small group of adult learners in a clinic or school setting is also a viable option.

The first 5 Listening and Talking Tools encourage children to listen carefully. The remaining 20 tools help children talk more and/or use more developed language skills. Each Listening and Talking Tool is described on a full page so that it can be explained and illustrated. You may want to make each page into an overhead transparency or scan it into a computer to make a Microsoft PowerPoint slide. Following every four or five strategies, a summary page is provided that presents previously taught strategies on one page. These summary pages are useful when reviewing strategies with adults. Adults may find the summary pages more useful to display in prominent locations because they take up less space by presenting several strategies at once.

Several Listening and Talking Tools should be presented during a single meeting. Depending on the length of the meetings, determine the number of strategies that need to be taught each time so that all 25 Listening and Talking Tools can be covered in an 8- to 12-week period. Previously taught strategies should be reviewed during each meeting. The summary pages that are provided throughout Chapter 1 make reviewing easy. In addition, other topics and agenda items (e.g., an IEP meeting, upcoming health visit schedule, or preschool options) may be addressed during these meeting times.

Children may or may not be present during the Listening and Talking Tools instruction. Depending on the number of adults present, the demands of the children, and the amount of time set aside for the meeting, determine whether children should be a part of all, some, or none of the instruction. It might be most beneficial to have the children playing off to the side (under supervision) during the initial part of the instruction and meeting. Then children and adults can start to interact more as the educator demonstrates specific Listening and Talking Tools and as adults begin to try out new strategies. Carefully balance any benefits of the inclusion of children into the meetings against the needs of adult learners to devote their attention to strategy development and practice.

Listening Skills: An Introduction (page 21) and *Talking Skills: An Introduction* (page 28) should be photocopied and distributed to adults prior to presenting the Listening and Talking Tools. These pages provide background information regarding the importance of children's listening and talking skills. Read these pages aloud with the adults and welcome questions related to the information. Take time to make sure adults understand the information.

During each session, present adults with a copy of each page (either physically or via an overhead or Microsoft PowerPoint slide) that contains a targeted Listening and Talking Tool. As with the introductory pages, read each strategy page aloud and invite questions. Using children or other adults, take time to demonstrate and/or role-play each new Listening and Talking Tool. If possible, have adults practice new strategies by role-playing with each other or with children. Provide constructive feedback as needed. Strongly encourage adults to use the new strategies during all of their interactions with children. Continually remind them about the positive effects of using each Listening and Talking Tool.

While helping adults learn the Listening and Talking Tools, be sure to assign activities for adults to conduct with children so that they can practice new strategies during non-meeting times. Activities from throughout Chapters 2–4 and from Part II are useful for this purpose. (Note that Chapters 2–4 include reproducible pages containing background information that should precede assigning the activities from those chapters.) Also provide adults with one copy of the *Review Page* (Appendix B, page 131) for each assigned activity. Encourage them to use the *Review Page* to summarize the activity, to tell how easy or hard it was to use the selected Listening and Talking Tools, and to reflect on how the child responded to their use of the tools.

Have the adults take all reproducible pages with them after each meeting. At the beginning of each training meeting, take time for the adults to talk about the activities they completed. Encourage them to discuss their uses of the Listening and Talking Tools during the activities.

Listening Skills
An Introduction

Listening is essential to understanding. Many children have a natural ability to listen carefully. Some children have a hearing difficulty that presents a challenge for listening. Many other children hear just fine but need extra help developing their listening skills. Listening involves more than hearing ability.

Children who listen attentively can...

- Understand more information

- Comment on what they hear

- Ask questions about what is happening

Children need to have listening skills modeled for them. When adults demonstrate careful listening skills, children can learn from those models. Also, when adults listen carefully to children, children are given a chance to express their ideas, needs, and wants. In order to help children listen more carefully, the following tools are recommended:

Children will listen carefully if...

- They can hear adequately

- You talk more slowly

- You get their attention before you talk

- It is quiet

- You use short, simple sentences

Children will listen carefully if...

they can hear adequately.

- Have children's hearing checked.

- Have ear infections treated immediately.

- Follow doctors' directions.

Talk! Talk! Talk!

Children will listen carefully if...

you talk more slowly.

You... left...teddy...behind... the...couch.

- Use a slower rate.
- Pause whenever it sounds natural.
- Pause right before saying important ideas.
- Pause between sentences.

Talk! Talk! Talk!

Children will listen carefully if...

you get their attention before you talk.

- Call children by their names.

- Touch children when you say their names.

- Wait for children to show that you have their attention.

Michael... let's knock down the tower.

Talk! Talk! Talk!

Children will listen carefully if...

it is quiet.

- **Turn off the TV.**
- **Turn off the radio or stereo.**
- **Wait for any loud noises to pass.**

Talk! Talk! Talk!

Children will listen carefully if...

you use short, simple sentences.

Grandma made hot chocolate. It's in the kitchen.

Talk! Talk! Talk!

Listening and Talking
Tools to Help Children Listen Carefully

Summary

Children will listen carefully if...

They can hear adequately.

You get their attention before you talk.

You talk more slowly.

It is quiet.

You use short, simple sentences.

Talk! Talk! Talk!

Talking Skills
An Introduction

Most young children express their language by talking. In order for children to become effective language users, adults need to talk and talk and talk. Children who are surrounded by adults who talk to them develop more effective language skills.

Adults can talk about...

- The children's interests
- The children's actions
- Their own actions
- Other people's actions
- The things children see

Language is more than just words.
Language is used to...

- Share ideas
- Express feelings
- Give information
- Ask questions
- Describe events
- Solve problems
- Direct others
- Entertain
- Socialize with others
- Show imagination
- Refuse
- Learn

Adults must also be effective listeners in order for children to have opportunities to practice talking. The Listening and Talking Tools that encourage *children* to talk more also target talking and listening behaviors that *adults* should use. There are many strategies that help children use language and become better talkers. When adults use these tools, children experience many positive language models and become more effective communicators.

Talk! Talk! Talk!

Children will talk more if you...

- Look at their faces
- Wait a few seconds before you reply to what they say
- Take only one speaking turn at a time
- Show you are listening

- Talk about what you are doing
- Talk about what they are doing
- Talk about what they want to talk about
- Talk about what you see

- Use new words
- Repeat new words often
- Repeat part or all of their sentences in question form
- Repeat their sentences and add to them

- Help them by starting their sentences or filling in difficult words
- Model correct sentence forms
- Respond to their feelings
- Ask appropriate questions

- Avoid criticizing them
- Avoid pressuring them to talk
- Avoid interrupting them
- Avoid changing topics quickly

Talk! Talk! Talk!

Children will talk more if you...

look at their faces.

This is especially important when you are talking to children and when children are talking to you.

Children will talk more if you...

wait a few seconds before you reply to what they say.

I played with Joey at school today.

1...2... 3...4...5...

And we made the neatest building out of blocks.

This gives children a chance to add more or to ask a question.

Talk! Talk! Talk!

Children will talk more if you...

take only one speaking turn at a time.

This gives children a chance to talk.

Talk! Talk! Talk!

Children will talk more if you...

show you are listening.

- **Face your body toward children.**

- **Give appropriate eye contact.**

- **Nod your head.**

- **Make small comments like "Um-hmm," "Really?," and "Oh."**

Talk! Talk! Talk!

Listening and Talking
Tools to Help Children Talk

Summary 1

Children will talk more if you...

Look at their faces.

Wait a few seconds before you reply to what they say.

Take only one speaking turn at a time.

Show you are listening.

Talk! Talk! Talk!

Children will talk more if you...

talk about what you are doing.

I'm making soup for our guests for dinner.

Talk! Talk! Talk!

Children will talk more if you...

talk about what they are doing.

You're feeding the duck.

Talk! Talk! Talk!

Children will talk more if you...

talk about what they want to talk about.

Talk! Talk! Talk!

Children will talk more if you...

talk about what you see.

Look! The bunny is jumping over the puddle.

Talk! Talk! Talk!

Listening and Talking
Tools to Help Children Talk

Summary 2

Children will talk more if you...

Talk about what you are doing.

Talk about what they are doing.

Talk about what they want to talk about.

Talk about what you see.

Talk! Talk! Talk!

Children will talk more if you...

use new words.

The <u>ladybug</u> has wings.

Talk! Talk! Talk!

Children will talk more if you...

repeat new words often.

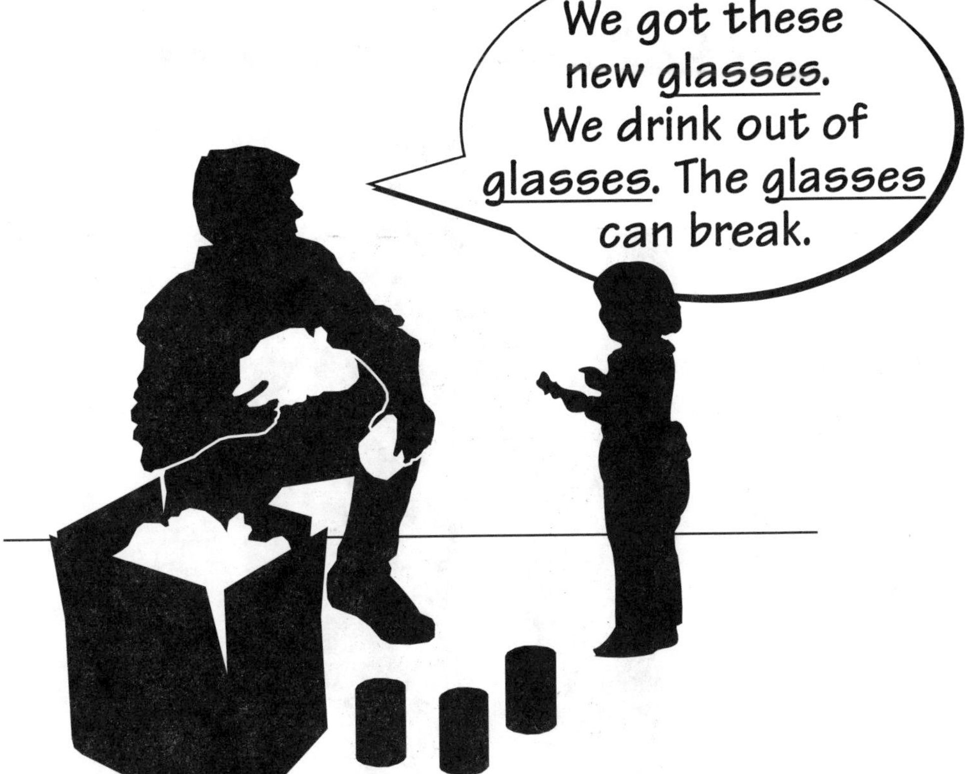

Children will talk more if you...

repeat part or all of their sentences in question form.

Talk! Talk! Talk!

Children will talk more if you...

repeat their sentences and add to them.

Talk! Talk! Talk!

Listening and Talking
Tools to Help Children Talk

Summary 3

Children will talk more if you...

Use new words.

Repeat new words often.

Repeat part or all of their sentences in question form.

Repeat their sentences and add to them.

Talk! Talk! Talk!

Children will talk more if you...

help them by starting their sentences or filling in difficult words.

Talk! Talk! Talk!

Children will talk more if you...

model correct sentence forms.

- **Speak slowly.**
- **Emphasize difficult sentence forms.**

Talk! Talk! Talk!

Children will talk more if you...

ask appropriate questions.

Talk! Talk! Talk!

Listening and Talking
Tools to Help Children Talk

Summary 4

Children will talk more if you...

Help them by starting their sentences or filling in difficult words.

Model correct sentence forms.

Respond to their feelings.

Ask appropriate questions.

Talk! Talk! Talk!

Children will talk more if you...

avoid pressuring them to talk.

Children will talk more if you...

avoid interrupting them.

Talk! Talk! Talk!

Children will talk more if you...

avoid changing topics quickly.

Talk! Talk! Talk!

Listening and Talking

Tools to Help Children Talk

Summary 5

Children will talk more if you...

Avoid criticizing them.

Avoid pressuring them to talk.

Avoid interrupting them.

Avoid changing topics quickly.

Talk! Talk! Talk!

Chapter 2

Scrapbooks

This chapter provides reproducible pages for teaching adults how to create and use scrapbooks with children to encourage speech and language development. The pictures and the written record contained on scrapbook pages provide scaffolding, or support, for children who may have difficulty expressing ideas verbally. Scrapbook pages help other people in children's lives understand what is important to a child and inquire about the details of a past event or story.

When explaining and modeling how to make scrapbook pages with adult learners, remember to illustrate how the Listening and Talking Tools can be incorporated. Also make every attempt to bring in samples of a variety of scrapbook pages. Adults will learn best when they can actually see what is meant by the different ideas.

Page 56 provides an overview that can be used as an overhead and/or handout during a meeting. Provide adults with a copy of the recommended Listening and Talking Tools for scrapbooks, outlined on page 57. Demonstrate each Listening and Talking Tool for adults.

Tell adults to help children include a variety of items in their scrapbooks including family photos, pictures children have drawn, and souvenirs. Adults should write down (i.e., print) their children's ideas or stories to go with the photos, pictures, and souvenirs on each scrapbook page. Encourage the use of scrapbooks to keep a record of therapy activities, school trips or events, special art projects, family events, and children's interests.

While adults are learning the basic set of Listening and Talking Tools presented in Chapter 1, focus on the topic of scrapbooks during one or several of the meetings. Initially, help the adults learn about the wide array of scrapbook options. Make them aware that simple scrapbook activities can lead to engaging conversations. Consider using some meeting time to help them get started making scrapbook pages with their children.

Provide adults with a copy of the *Review Page* in Appendix B (page 131) whenever a scrapbook activity is assigned. This page helps adults and children reflect on an experience after it has been conducted. Adults can be encouraged to return completed *Review Pages* to be discussed at follow-up meetings.

Scrapbooks

An Introduction

Scrapbooks can serve as personal diaries for children. They can be used to record important activities and experiences in children's lives. Scrapbooks are an easy way to remind children about past events. They are also useful as a way to help children tell stories and talk with others. Scrapbooks can be simple, but still help children use language.

Scrapbooks are useful for...

- Helping children describe events

- Helping children ask questions

- Teaching children new words

- Teaching concepts like colors, shapes, and sizes

- Improving sequencing skills by helping children tell stories in a logical order

- Helping children develop reading and writing skills

- Developing categorization skills (grouping things that go together)

Helping children make and use scrapbooks is a terrific way for you to practice the Listening and Talking Tools. Scrapbooks provide a useful record of Plan-Do-Review activities that you complete together. Children are proud to show their scrapbooks to others. When doing so, they are given the chance to talk, talk, talk!

The following information will help you get a better idea of how to create and use scrapbooks with children. Remember that imagination is important, so let the child lead the way. There are endless possibilities for creating and using scrapbooks!

Talk! Talk! Talk!

Scrapbooks
Listening and Talking Tools

When creating or looking at scrapbook pages with children, you can make the experience even more stimulating by using a variety of the Listening and Talking Tools. Using various tools allows children to hear and see appropriate language models and have the chance to use their own language skills.

Listening and Talking Tools to use with scrapbooks include...

- Talk more slowly

- Work in a quiet place

- Use short, simple sentences

- Talk about what you are doing

- Talk about what they are doing

- Talk about what you see

- Repeat their sentences and add to them

- Model correct sentence forms

- Ask appropriate questions

- Avoid criticizing them

Talk! Talk! Talk!

Creating Scrapbooks with Children

Scrapbooks are pages of memories bound together. There are a variety of scrapbook formats, including binders; blank journals; photo albums; or pages secured with binder rings, string, staples, or paper clips.

In addition to materials that hold the pages together, the following supplies are useful when creating scrapbook pages:

- Scissors
- Souvenirs
- Pens and pencils
- Photographs
- Stencils
- Page protectors
- Stickers
- Markers
- Glue or tape
- Crayons
- Construction paper
- Magazines/Catalogs

Consider keeping a kit of scrapbook supplies handy. Any storage container can be used as a scrapbook kit. Keeping all the supplies in one place makes it easier to create scrapbook pages.

Construction paper; photo album pages; or any other blank, sturdy surface can serve as the background for each scrapbook page. When using less-sturdy background pages, consider inserting completed scrapbook pages into page protectors to keep them safe.

Photographs make a terrific addition to any scrapbook page. Keep a loaded camera handy at all times to help make sure you have lots of pictures to use when creating future scrapbook pages. Consider keeping disposable cameras in key locations (e.g., at a grandparent's house or in the car) so that pictures can be taken during a variety of situations. Taking pictures of children becomes automatic with a little practice. Consider having duplicate photographs made when having film developed. This provides one copy of each picture to use for scrapbooks and one copy to keep in a more traditional photo album.

Talk! Talk! Talk!

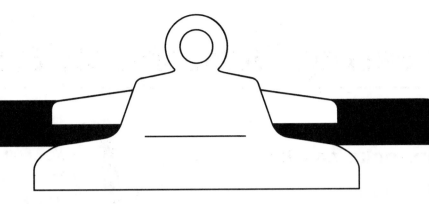

Helping Children Create a Scrapbook Page

1. After determining the topic for a page, help children select photographs, magazine and catalog pictures, stickers, souvenirs, and any other materials that will go on the page.

2. Assist children with cutting out any necessary items so that all desired pieces fit on the page. Use more than one page if necessary.

3. Help children glue or tape the selected items onto the page.

4. Help children add extra details and decorations to the page if they want.

5. Have children dictate descriptions, stories, captions, or dialogue to accompany the pictures and other items on the page. Write the words children use near each item.

6. If necessary, allow the page to dry and/or place the page into a page protector. Add the page to the scrapbook.

Creating Scrapbook Pages

Scrapbooks can include...

- Photographs from home or school

"Jackson went down the slide."

"I went to see Mary's play.
It had a funny clown."

- Souvenirs, or other items, from a family trip, a school field trip, or a special event

"Toys I want for
my birthday."

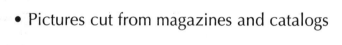

- Pictures cut from magazines and catalogs

"Mom and Dad went to visit Nana."

- Drawings and artwork created by children

NOTE: Various arts and crafts materials can also be used to decorate the scrapbook pages.

Talk! Talk! Talk!

Creating and Talking About Scrapbooks

Scrapbooks are useful for...

Helping children describe events

When creating or looking at a scrapbook page with children, talk about what happened, who was there, and how people felt. Have children dictate words that can be written on the scrapbook page. Ask children questions about the pictures and items on the page, such as...

- What happened?
- Who was there?

- Where was it?
- How did you feel?

Helping children ask questions

Use photographs and objects that are interesting to children and that will spark them to ask questions. Allow time for children to ask about the photographs and objects.

Teaching children new words

When creating or looking at a scrapbook page, name and describe people and objects that appear in pictures. Always provide labels and descriptions for words that are new to children. After helping children learn a new word, give them a chance to use the new word by asking questions.

Creating and Talking About Scrapbooks

Scrapbooks are useful for...

Teaching concepts like colors, shapes, and sizes

When creating or looking at a scrapbook page, provide appropriate descriptions and labels for concepts. If descriptions are clear, children will learn more about an object. Important concepts for young children include...

- Colors ("That is red. Red is a nice color to use to draw an apple.")
- Shapes ("Look, the pool at school is shaped like a rectangle.")
- Sizes ("Oh boy, the snowman's head is bigger than his bottom.")

Improving sequencing skills

Scrapbook pages that show an event in sequence are a great way to help a child tell a story. Give the child a turn to explain the sequences depicted in the pictures on scrapbook pages. For example,

Helping children develop reading and writing skills

Be sure to include a written description for items on each scrapbook page. Ideally, children should dictate the words to go on the page. Let children add their own writing to the page. Children love to "read" scrapbook pages that they have written.

Talk! Talk! Talk!

Scrapbooks are useful for...

Developing categorization skills

Scrapbook pages can be created to show a specific category of objects. Using photographs, stickers, stencils, and pictures cut from catalogs and magazines, category pages can be created.

Here are two examples.

Category Suggestions

clothes	cold things	vegetables
colors	trucks	animals
drinks	cereals	footwear
TV shows	hats	hot things
cartoon characters	hard things	storybook characters
weather	pets	body parts
soft things	jobs	things on your face
buildings	furniture	tools
funny things	sports	dogs
desserts	fruits	things in a circus
holidays	dangerous things	insects
things made of wood	kitchen items	round things
transportation	paper products	things on the playground
cleaning products	tiny things	musical instruments

Chapter 3

Stories

This chapter provides reproducible pages for helping adults learn about the importance of reading, telling, and writing stories with children in order to encourage speech and language development. The objective of this chapter is to help adults use stories in a more interactive way.

Keep a variety of children's books around for adults to review. Consider having a lending library available so that parents can borrow literature to use with children. Remember to model the use of story reading, storytelling, and story writing as an effective language facilitation process.

The overview, provided on page 66, can be used as an overhead and/or handout during a meeting. The story structure guide, provided on page 67, can be used as an overhead and/or handout to help adults better understand the parts of a traditional story. Provide adult learners with copies of the recommended Listening and Talking Tools for stories, outlined on page 68. Demonstrate each Listening and Talking Tool for the adults.

Encourage adults to save children's written stories. Mention that stories make excellent additions to scrapbook pages. Encourage adults to elicit stories that relate to special events in children's lives, such as outings, visits to friends and relatives, or trips to restaurants. Also provide adults with a copy of the steps to follow when engaging in story activities with the child as outlined on pages 69–72.

While teaching the basic set of Listening and Talking Tools presented in Chapter 1, consider structuring at least one meeting agenda to focus on the topic of stories. Consider using meeting time to model storytelling skills and to provide adult learners with opportunities to read and tell stories to children.

Provide adults with a copy of the *Review Page* in Appendix B (page 131) whenever a story activity is assigned. This page helps adults and children reflect on the experience after it has been conducted. Adults can be encouraged to return completed *Review Pages* to be discussed at follow-up meetings.

Stories

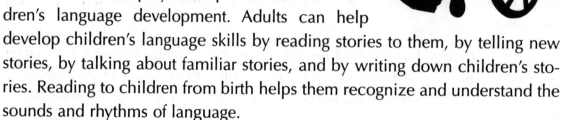

An Introduction

Books and stories play an important role in children's language development. Adults can help develop children's language skills by reading stories to them, by telling new stories, by talking about familiar stories, and by writing down children's stories. Reading to children from birth helps them recognize and understand the sounds and rhythms of language.

When listening to stories, children increase their vocabulary skills, learn about the way language is structured, discover how to tell a story in the correct order, learn how to guess what will happen next, and develop the skills they need to become skilled readers. Reading to children every day helps them develop these skills.

When selecting books to read to children, choose from a variety of books that...

- Help children use their imaginations and talk about their ideas, wishes, fears, and interests

- Have interesting pictures, to help capture and maintain their interest

- Are repetitive, to help children learn new sentence structures

- Are humorous or captivating, to help children develop a desire to listen and to tell their own stories

- Contain only pictures, to help children develop the ability to tell their own stories and to talk about the pictures and actions shown in the book

- Are about things the child knows or is interested in and encourage the child to talk about his or her own interests and experiences

Talk! Talk! Talk!

Stories

Story Structure

Children will understand, tell, and write better stories when they understand the various parts of a story. The questions you ask when reading, telling, and writing stories with children can help them learn these important story parts. Ask children the following questions when you read, tell, and write stories together.

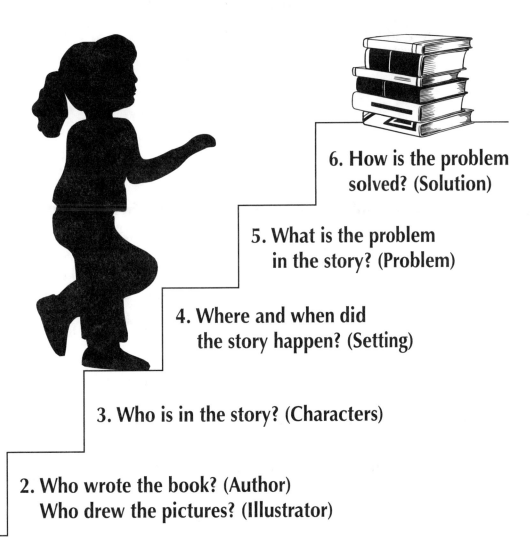

6. How is the problem solved? (Solution)

5. What is the problem in the story? (Problem)

4. Where and when did the story happen? (Setting)

3. Who is in the story? (Characters)

2. Who wrote the book? (Author)
   Who drew the pictures? (Illustrator)

1. What is the name of the book? (Title)

Talk! Talk! Talk!

Stories
Listening and Talking Tools

When *reading, telling,* and *writing* stories with children...

• Read and talk slowly

• Make sure to say each word

• Be sure to have their attention

• Find a quiet place to read

• Use short, simple sentences in stories you tell and write

• Talk about the pictures you see in a book

• Use their ideas for the stories you tell and write

• Use new words and explain their meanings

• Repeat what they say, modeling correct words and sentence structure

• Start a familiar sentence and then stop to see if they can finish the sentence

• Model sentences that could be used in the story

• Ask questions about the story and pictures

• Avoid criticizing their ideas and sentences

• Avoid interrupting them when they are telling a story

Talk! Talk! Talk!

Reading Books to Children

Reading to children will...

- Increase language development
- Improve listening skills
- Develop reading-readiness skills

General Suggestions

- Start at birth and continue even after children know how to read. Children are never too young or too old to be read to.

- Visit the library often.

- Attend story time at local bookstores.

- Give books as gifts.

- Be a reader yourself. Let children see you read for pleasure.

- Talk about the parts of the book—title, author, illustrator, characters, setting, problem, solution, front, back, beginning, ending.

- Read favorite books over and over and let children fill in words they know.

- Hold the book so that children can see it. Move your finger along under the words as you read them.

- Read every day.

- Leave books around the house or room.

- Talk about the pictures in the book.

- Look at the pictures first and have children try to guess what might happen.

- Sit close together while holding the book.

Talk! Talk! Talk!

Telling Stories to Children

Telling stories to children will...

- Develop language skills

- Improve listening skills

- Increase storytelling skills

- Heighten imagination

General Suggestions

- Stories can be about:

    Family events—"I am going to tell you a story about what we are going to do next weekend."

    Pets—"This is a story about a kitten named Whiskers."

    Childhood memories—"This story is about my first trip to the zoo."

    Trips or vacations—"This story is about the time we went camping."

- Stories can take the form of:

    Fairy tales, such as "Cinderella"

    Myths, such as "How the Leopard Got His Spots"

    Fables or fantasy stories, such as "The Wizard of Oz"

    Nursery rhymes, such as "Mary Had a Little Lamb"

- Stories can be long or short, as long as all the important parts are included.

- Tell stories to children AND have children tell stories to you.

Talk! Talk! Talk!

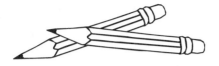

Writing Stories with Children

Writing stories with children will...

- Increase language development

- Improve storytelling skills

- Heighten imagination

- Develop reading-readiness skills

General Suggestions

- Write stories with children to help them understand that a book is a story that can be written down and saved.

- Use blank or lined pages to make books to write stories in.

- Have children tell the stories while you write the words.

- Encourage children to illustrate their stories.

- Have children read their stories after they are written. Encourage them to read their stories to many people.

- Save the books children create. Take the stories out from time to time for children to read.

Talk! Talk! Talk!

20 Minutes a Day

Read to your children
Twenty minutes a day;
You have the time,
And so do they.

Read while the laundry is in the machine;
Read while the dinner cooks;
Tuck a child in the crook of your arm
And reach for the library books.

Hide the remote,
Let the computer games cool,
For one day your children will be off to school;
"Remedial?" "Gifted?" You have the choice;
Let them hear their first tales
In the sound of your voice.

Read in the morning;
Read over noon;
Read by the light of
Good Night Moon.

Turn the pages together,
Sitting close as you'll fit.
Till a small voice beside you says,
"Hey, don't quit."

—Richard Peck
(printed with permission)

Talk! Talk! Talk!

Chapter 4

Television and Videos

This chapter provides reproducible pages for helping adults learn how to include appropriate television and video programs in children's lives. Electronic media are a major influence in the lives of today's children; computer games, music videos, movies, and television surround children in our society. It is not being suggested that such media encourage good communication skills. Adults should be urged to limit a child's exposure to such sources. However, children will continue to encounter television and video in their daily lives, and there are many strategies that can make experiences with electronic media more meaningful.

The American Academy of Pediatrics (AAP) released a policy statement that offers television viewing guidelines for young children. Adults are urged to avoid television for children under 2 years of age and to keep children's rooms "electronic media-free" (AAP, 1995a). The AAP indicated that the average child watches 21 to 23 hours of television per week (excluding videotaped programs). Children's television viewing should be limited to 1 to 2 hours per day (AAP, 1995b).

The strategies in this chapter are designed for adults to use while watching television with children. A variety of objectives can be targeted using these strategies: (1) stimulate conversation related to the program between adults and children, (2) help make children more critical viewers of the programs they watch, (3) scaffold a language activity while watching a program to help children learn new concepts and skills, and (4) foreshadow and review parts of the program to help children understand and retell the story plot and sequence.

The overview, provided on pages 74–75, can be used as overheads and/or handouts to introduce this topic during a meeting. Pages 76–79 can be distributed as assignments to guide adults' television and video viewing time with children. While no specific Listening and Talking Tools are highlighted in this chapter, adults should be encouraged to use all appropriate tools while watching programs with children.

Demonstrate and role-play the techniques provided within this chapter to adults during a meeting time. Consider having adults keep notes about the programs they watch with children and children's general television habits. Use meeting time to have adults share their notes and talk about how they modified television and video viewing with children.

Provide adults with a copy of the *Review Page* in Appendix B (page 131) whenever a television or video activity is assigned. This page helps adults and children reflect on an experience after it has been conducted. Adults can be encouraged to return completed *Review Pages* to be discussed at follow-up meetings.

Television & Videos
An Introduction

Electronic entertainment is a major influence in the lives of children. Television, movies, and computer games surround children in our society every day. These activities can be learning tools, but the American Academy of Pediatrics (AAP) warns adults to be careful about the amount and the types of programs and movies their children see. In 1995, they warned that excessive viewing of the wrong types of programs could contribute to violent behavior, obesity, early sexual activity, drug and alcohol use and abuse, poor school performance and ethnic stereotyping.

According to Neilson data from 1993, most American children spend more hours watching television than any other activity, besides sleeping and going to school.[1] By the time they reach age 70, it can add up to 7 to 10 years of television watching.[2] The AC Neilson Company reported that the average child watches 21 to 23 hours of television per week (not including video watching). The AAP recommends children's daily television viewing be limited to 1 to 2 hours per day.[3]

Electronic entertainment does not encourage good communication skills, so adults are urged to limit children's exposure to television and videos. There are many strategies to make the best possible use of television and videos for developing speech and language skills in children. Most importantly, children should be with an adult when watching television and videotaped movies. Adults can then use recommended strategies to make the most of the programs or movies children are viewing.

1. AC Neilson Company. (1993). *The 1992–1993 report on television.* New York, Nielson Media Research.

2. Strasburger, V.C. (1993). Children, adolescents, and the media: Five crucial issues. *Adolescent Media: State of the Art Review, 4,* 479–493.

3. American Academy of Pediatrics Committee on Communications. (1995). Children, adolescents, and television. *Pediatrics, 96*(Suppl. 4), 786–787.

Talk! Talk! Talk!

Television and Videos
Setting Guidelines for Children

The guide *Caring for Your School-Aged Child: Ages 5 to 12* (AAP, 1995) offers useful suggestions for parents. Parents are urged to avoid television for children under 2 years of age and to keep children's rooms "electronic media-free" (AAP, 1995).

The American Academy of Pediatrics offers the following specific ways for caregivers to keep children's TV viewing in balance...

- Set limits on the amount of TV children watch (no more than 2 hours per day)

- Help children plan TV viewing in advance

- Know what TV shows children watch

- Do not permit TV watching during mealtime

- Do not allow children to have a TV set in their bedroom

- Keep books, magazines, and board games near the TV set

- Limit your own TV watching to set a good example

- Ask local TV stations to carry educational programs for children

- Unplug the TV if it causes arguments or fights

American Academy of Pediatrics. (1995). *Caring for your school-aged child: Ages 5 to 12*. New York: Bantam.

Television and Videos

Making it Meaningful

Children learn language best by talking with adults and other children. Watching television does not develop a children's language unless adults watch with them and talk about the following story elements:

 Who was in the show?

 When did the show take place?

 Where did the show take place?

 What was the problem?

 How was the problem solved?

NOTE: If you can't watch a program with children, ask them to tell you about it later.

Talk! Talk! Talk!

Television and Videos
Making it Meaningful

Children learn language best by talking with adults and other children. Watching television does not develop children's language unless adults watch with them.

Talk about what is real and what is not real.
Ask the following questions...

Could that really happen?

Is there such a thing?

Has that ever happened to you?

NOTE: Use time during commercials to talk about what is happening in the show and what might happen next.

Talk! Talk! Talk!

Television and Videos
Making it Meaningful

Children learn language best by talking with adults and other children. Watching television does not develop children's language unless adults watch with them.

**Talk about the characters in the show.
Ask the following questions...**

How do the characters feel?

Why do the characters feel that way?

What do you like about the different characters?
What don't you like?

Which character would you like to be? Why?

Television and Videos
Making it Meaningful

Children learn language best by talking with adults and other children. Watching television does not develop children's language unless adults watch with them.

Talk about what your child learned.

Talk about new words used in the show.

Encourage your child to ask you what words mean.

Have your child watch educational shows like:
Sesame Street
Zoom
The Magic School Bus
Bill Nye, the Science Guy

Encourage your child to read books related to favorite shows.

Part II

Plan-Do-Review
Activities

Plan-Do-Review

The Plan-Do-Review activities suggested in Part II provide parents with the opportunity to practice using Listening and Talking Tools while interacting with children. Provide a copy of pages 84–85 as an introduction to the Plan-Do-Review activities. These pages explain and illustrate the Plan-Do-Review activities and their importance. Read these pages aloud and discuss the information provided. Respond to adults' questions.

At the end of each meeting, present at least two different Plan-Do-Review activity pages for adults to use with children. Provide adults with one copy of the *Review Page* in Appendix B (page 131) for each assigned Plan-Do-Review activity. The *Review Page* is a tool for parents to use with their children when conducting the review component of the activities. Encourage adults to conduct all assigned Plan-Do-Review activities prior to the next meeting time.

When adults return completed *Review Pages,* take time to review them together. Have adults describe the language skills that were targeted and the Listening and Talking Tools that were practiced during the activity. If children are present, encourage them to refer to the picture created on the *Review Page* when talking about the activity. These pages serve as a helpful way for you to provide feedback to adults.

The *Plan-Do-Review Activity Worksheet* on page 86 can be used in two ways. As one option, this page should be photocopied and distributed to adults to use as a guide for assigned Plan-Do-Review activities. Adults should use this sheet to outline target words and target Listening and Talking Tools for each assigned activity. By completing this sheet and keeping it accessible throughout the activity, adults can be reminded of all three steps (i.e., Plan, Do, Review). As another option, adults can be encouraged to use this form to create their own Plan-Do-Review activities. Consider making this option available to adults when an assigned Plan-Do-Review activity is not appropriate. In addition, consider using adult meeting time to help adults create and outline original Plan-Do-Review activities.

Plan-Do-Review Activities
An Introduction

Plan-Do-Review activities are easy to do. They use common, everyday situations for two purposes:

- To give children chances to learn and practice their new language skills

- To help adults practice the Listening and Talking Tools

Each activity gives suggestions for new words to teach a child and for Listening and Talking Tools to practice. You are able to decide which words and sentence forms to target with a child and which strategies to practice.

The three steps to every Plan-Do-Review activity are as follows...

1. Plan

- Select words (or sentence forms) you want the child to learn or practice during the activity.

- Choose the Listening and Talking Tools you want to practice during the activity.

- Gather any materials that are needed.

2. Do

- Conduct the activity.

- Use the Listening and Talking Tools during the entire activity.

3. Review

- Follow the directions for each activity review.

- Complete a *Review Page* with the child.

- Conduct one or both of the recommended "Extension Activities" to give the child another chance to hear and use the targeted words and to provide more opportunities for you to practice the Listening and Talking Tools.

Talk! Talk! Talk!

Plan-Do-Review

Example

Plan	Do	Review

Plan: We're going to go for a walk to the park, and we'll pick different leaves.

Do: We're walking in the park. See the oak leaves?

Review: We went to the park. We picked some oak leaves.

Mom told me you went to the park today.

This shows a small portion of each step of a sample Plan-Do-Review activity.

Talk! Talk! Talk!

Plan-Do-Review
Activity Worksheet

Plan

Activity name:

_____

New words to target:

- _____   - _____
- _____   - _____
- _____   - _____

Listening and Talking Tools to practice:

- _____
- _____
- _____

Materials needed: _____

_____

_____

Do

Describe the activity: _____

_____

_____

Review

Complete the *Review Page.* How else will we review the activity?

☐ Draw a picture sequence   ☐ Create a scrapbook page

☐ Tell or write a longer story ☐ Tell someone about what we did

☐ Other: _____

Talk! Talk! Talk!

Plan-Do-Review Activities

Outdoors

Seasons

Transportation

Furry-Creature First Aid

Plan

- Select words you want the child to learn (e.g., *bandage, tape, hospital, doctor, nurse, shoulder*). List these words on the *Plan-Do-Review Activity Worksheet* to serve as a reminder during the activity.

- Select Listening and Talking Tools to practice. List these strategies on the *Plan-Do-Review Activity Worksheet* to serve as a reminder during the activity.

- Gather a first-aid kit and a variety of stuffed animals.

Do

- Talk to the child about what you will be doing together. Explain the sequence of events. For example, "We are going to pretend the stuffed animals are sick and hurt. First we will take care of the dog. Then we will help the bear. Last we will fix the elephant. We will use bandages and medicine."

- Help the child use the first-aid materials with the stuffed animals.

- Use Listening and Talking Tools when talking with the child as you play. For example:

  Talk about what you are doing—"I am rolling the gauze around his leg."

  Talk about what the child is doing—"You are cutting the tape."

  Use new words—"The bear hurt his *shoulder.*"

Review

- Immediately after the activity, talk about what happened. For example, "Today we pretended to help the stuffed animals. We helped the dog, then the bear, then the elephant. They feel better now." Complete a *Review Page.*

- Have the child draw a picture of the activity for a scrapbook page and write or tell a story about what happened. Encourage the child to show the picture or tell the story to another person (e.g., a sibling, a grandparent).

Extension Activities
- Read a book with the child about going to the doctor or taking a pet to the vet.
- Have the child come along on a trip to the vet.

Potato Animals

Plan

- Select words you want the child to learn (e.g., *arm, leg, trunk, tail, big, little, sharp)*. List these words on the *Plan-Do-Review Activity Worksheet* to serve as a reminder during the activity.

- Select Listening and Talking Tools to practice. List these strategies on the *Plan-Do-Review Activity Worksheet* to serve as a reminder during the activity.

- Gather several whole potatoes, a variety of potato pieces cut to look like animal parts, toothpicks, and several small jelly candies.

Do

- Talk to the child about what you will be doing together. Explain the sequence of events. For example, "We are going to make a potato animal. We will use a potato for the body. Then we will use potato pieces for some body parts. Then we will use candy for the really small body parts."

- Help the child use the toothpicks to attach various potato pieces and jelly candies to the body.

- Use Listening and Talking Tools when talking with the child as you create a potato animal together. For example:

  Make sure that it is quiet—Complete this activity in a quiet location.

  Take only one speaking turn at a time—"I will use this piece for the nose."

  Avoid criticizing the child—"Good try, but that's an ear. That's a tough one to figure out."

Review

- Immediately after the activity, talk about what happened. For example, "Today we made a potato animal. We used potatoes and candy to make an elephant. When we were done, we took a picture of the elephant." Complete a *Review Page*.

- Have the child draw a picture of the activity for a scrapbook page and write or tell a story about what happened. Encourage the child to show the picture or tell the story to another person (e.g., a sibling, a grandparent).

Extension Activities
- Talk about how potatoes can be prepared (e.g., baked, boiled, mashed).
- Draw animals on construction paper with paint, crayons, or markers.

Zoo Time

Plan

- Select words you want the child to learn (e.g., animal names, *cage, den, cave, pond)*. List these words on the *Plan-Do-Review Activity Worksheet* to serve as a reminder during the activity.

- Select Listening and Talking Tools to practice. List these strategies on the *Plan-Do-Review Activity Worksheet* to serve as a reminder during the activity.

Do

- Talk to the child about what you will be doing together. Explain the sequence of events. For example, "We are going to go to the zoo. First we will drive to the zoo. When we get to the zoo, we will see lots of animals. We will eat lunch at the zoo. Last we will drive home from the zoo."

- Take the child to the zoo.

- Use Listening and Talking Tools when talking with the child as you go through the zoo. For example:

  Use short, simple sentences—"We are at the zoo. The zoo is big. The zoo is busy."

  Talk about what you see—"I see a monkey."

  Ask appropriate questions—"Is the lion sleeping?"

Review

- Immediately after the activity, talk about what happened. For example, "Today we went to the zoo. We had fun looking at the animals. We had pizza for lunch at the zoo. You fell asleep on our way back." Or you can talk about what you saw first, next, and last. Complete a *Review Page.*

- Have the child draw a picture of the activity for a scrapbook page and write or tell a story about what happened. Encourage the child to show the picture or tell the story to another person (e.g., a sibling, a grandparent).

Extension Activities

- Take the child to visit a farm, a pet store, or a local animal shelter.
- Read the child books about zoo animals.

Cardboard House

Plan

- Select words you want the child to learn (e.g., *door, roof, wall, window, open, close).* List these words on the *Plan-Do-Review Activity Worksheet* to serve as a reminder during the activity.

- Select Listening and Talking Tools to practice. List these strategies on the *Plan-Do-Review Activity Worksheet* to serve as a reminder during the activity.

- Gather a large cardboard box (e.g., one for a large appliance); a knife, saw, or scissors; and markers or paint.

Do

- Talk to the child about what you will be doing together. Explain the sequence of events. For example, "We are going to make a cardboard house. First we will cut out a door and windows. Then we can color the house. When it's done, we can play in the house."

- Cut a large flap for the door. Cut window openings. (Be sure the child is not left alone with the cutting tool.) Help the child color or paint the house. Suggest drawing such things as a door knob, flowers, and a house number.

- Use Listening and Talking Tools when talking with the child as you work. For example:

  Talk about what the child is doing—"You are painting the door green."

  Repeat the child's sentences and add to them—*"It's a saw.* The saw is sharp."

  Respond to the child's feelings—"Are you upset you can't use the saw? The saw is too sharp. You can use the markers."

Review

- Immediately after the activity, talk about what happened. For example, "We made a cardboard house. I used the knife to cut out the door and windows. Then we painted the house green." Complete a *Review Page.*

- Have the child draw a picture of the activity for a scrapbook page and write or tell a story about what happened. Encourage the child to show the picture or tell the story to another person (e.g., a sibling, a grandparent).

Extension Activities
- Make a car out of a smaller cardboard box.
- Make houses for stuffed animals and dolls using small cardboard boxes.

Cleaning the Kitchen

Plan

- Select words you want the child to learn (e.g., *hot, sponge, scrub, floor, table*). List these words on the *Plan-Do-Review Activity Worksheet* to serve as a reminder during the activity.

- Select Listening and Talking Tools to practice. List these strategies on the *Plan-Do-Review Activity Worksheet* to serve as a reminder during the activity.

- Gather a variety of cleaning supplies.

Do

- Talk to the child about what you will be doing together. Explain the sequence of events. For example, "We are going to clean today. First we will wash the table. Then we will wipe off the chairs. We will use hot, soapy water and a sponge. Last we can sweep the floor together."

- Work with the child to clean the kitchen.

- Use Listening and Talking Tools when talking with the child as you clean. For example:

    Get the child's attention before giving each new direction—"Elizabeth, try this one."

    Repeat part or all of the child's sentences in question form—"Where is the *sponge?*"

    Repeat new words often—"We *scrubbed* with the sponge. We *scrubbed* the table. Then we *scrubbed* the chairs."

Review

- Immediately after the activity, talk about what happened. For example, "Today we cleaned the kitchen together. We used hot water to clean the table and chairs. After that we swept the floor." Complete a *Review Page*.

- Have the child draw a picture of the activity for a scrapbook page and write or tell a story about what happened. Encourage the child to show the picture or tell the story to another person (e.g., a sibling, a grandparent).

Extension Activities
- Help the child clean his or her bedroom.
- Have the child help you wash the inside and outside of a car.

Flashlight Fun

Plan

- Select words you want the child to learn (e.g., *flashlight, on, off, in, under, up, down, dark, light*). List these words on the *Plan-Do-Review Activity Worksheet* to serve as a reminder during the activity.

- Select Listening and Talking Tools to practice. List these strategies on the *Plan-Do-Review Activity Worksheet* to serve as a reminder during the activity.

- Gather one or more flashlights.

Do

- Talk to the child about what you will be doing together. Explain the sequence of events. For example, "We are going to play with flashlights. First we will make the room dark. Then we will turn on our flashlights. We will find things in the room and talk about what we find."

- Darken the room and help the child explore with the flashlight. Talk about items as they are found with the flashlight.

- Use Listening and Talking Tools when talking with the child as you play together. For example:

  Take only one speaking turn at a time—"I see a book on top of the TV. What do you see?"

  Ask appropriate questions—"Can you find the ball?"

  Avoid changing topics quickly—After finding an item with the flashlight, talk about it for a while before searching for the next item.

Review

- Immediately after the activity, talk about what happened. For example: "Today we played a flashlight game. We found the book on top of the TV. We found my shoes under the table. Last we used the flashlight to find the light switch." Complete a *Review Page*.

- Have the child draw a picture of the activity for a scrapbook page and write or tell a story about what happened. Encourage the child to show the picture or tell the story to another person (e.g., a sibling, a grandparent).

Extension Activities

- Read a book with the child that talks about the locations of objects.
- Model location words whenever finding objects with the child.

Talk! Talk! Talk!

Laundry Time

Plan

- Select words you want the child to learn (e.g., *clean, dirty, cold, warm, hot, wash, dry, sort*). List these words on the *Plan-Do-Review Activity Worksheet* to serve as a reminder during the activity.

- Select Listening and Talking Tools to practice. List these strategies on the *Plan-Do-Review Activity Worksheet* to serve as a reminder during the activity.

- Gather laundry soap, fabric softener, dirty clothes, and a laundry basket.

Do

- Talk to the child about what you will be doing together. Explain the sequence of events. For example, "We are going to do laundry together. First we will sort the clothes. Then we will wash the clothes. Then we will dry the clothes. Last we will fold the clothes and put them away."

- Have the child help you sort, wash, dry, fold, and put away a load of clothes. Help the child put the clothes in the washing machine and add soap, put the clothes in the dryer, fold small items, and put the clothes away.

- Use Listening and Talking Tools when talking with the child as you work together to do a load of laundry. For example:

  Talk about what you are doing—"I am taking the clothes out of the dryer."

  Help the child by filling in difficult words—"That is *detergent.*"

  Use new words—"We need to *sort* the clothes first."

Review

- Immediately after the activity, talk about what happened. For example, "Today we did laundry. We sorted the clothes first. Then we washed a load of jeans. I put the jeans in the dryer. We folded the jeans together. Last we put the jeans away." Complete a *Review Page.*

- Have the child draw a picture of the activity for a scrapbook page and write or tell a story about what happened. Encourage the child to show the picture or tell the story to another person (e.g., a sibling, a grandparent).

Extension Activities
- Visit a laundromat or a dry cleaner with the child.
- Wash, dry, and put away dishes with the child.

Lid Match

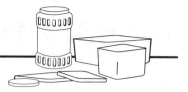

Plan

- Select words you want the child to learn (e.g., *big, little, push, pull, turn, twist, short, tall, empty, full*). List these words on the *Plan-Do-Review Activity Worksheet* to serve as a reminder during the activity.

- Select Listening and Talking Tools to practice. List these strategies on the *Plan-Do-Review Activity Worksheet* to serve as a reminder during the activity.

- Gather a variety of storage containers with their matching lids.

Do

- Talk to the child about what you will be doing together. Explain the sequence of events. For example, "We are going to put a lid on each container. First we will put the big lids on the big containers. Then we will put the little lids on the little containers. We have many containers and lids to look at."

- Help the child try different lids on different containers until every container has a lid.

- Use Listening and Talking Tools when talking with the child as you play together. For example:

  Talk slowly—"This container is big." (pause) "This lid is not big."

  Look at the child in the face.

  Respond to the child's feelings—"Are you upset that the lid doesn't fit?"

Review

- Immediately after the activity, talk about what happened. For example, "Today we matched lids and containers. We had nine containers and lids. We found all the matches." Complete a *Review Page*.

- Have the child draw a picture of the activity for a scrapbook page and write or tell a story about what happened. Encourage the child to show the picture or tell the story to another person (e.g., a sibling, a grandparent).

Extension Activities

- Use materials (e.g., cotton balls, LEGOs, dry beans) to fill the various containers.
- Play other matching games with the child (e.g., pairing up socks, matching objects with their locations).

Talk! Talk! Talk!

Television Talk

Plan

- Select words you want the child to learn (e.g., *beginning, end, where, when, who, real, pretend*). List these words on the *Plan-Do-Review Activity Worksheet* to serve as a reminder during the activity.

- Select Listening and Talking Tools to practice. List these strategies on the *Plan-Do-Review Activity Worksheet* to serve as a reminder during the activity.

Do

- Talk to the child about what you will be doing together. Explain the sequence of events if you know it. For example, "We are going to watch a show together. The show is about a girl named Jody. Jody gets a new bike. It is hard for her to ride the bike. Jody gets help from her brother. Let's watch the show about Jody and her bike."

- Watch a show with the child. During commercials, turn the volume down and talk about what has happened and what might happen next.

- Use Listening and Talking Tools when talking with the child as you watch a television show together. For example:

  Get the child's attention before you talk—"Heather, do you like Jody's bike?"

  Repeat new words often—"Jody has a pet *hamster*. The *hamster* is small."

  Ask appropriate questions—"Why is Jody happy?"

Review

- Immediately after the activity, talk about what happened. For example, "Today we watched a show together. It was a funny show about a girl named Jody and her new bike. Jody learned how to ride her bike. It was a great show!" Complete a *Review Page*.

- Have the child draw a picture of the show for a scrapbook page and write or tell a story about what happened. Encourage the child to show the picture or tell the story to another person (e.g., a sibling, a grandparent).

Extension Activities
- Read a book to the child that is related to the show you watched together.
- Act out a scene from a show with the child.

Touch and Feel Game

Plan

- Select words you want the child to learn (e.g., names of objects, *soft, rough, smooth, bumpy, big, little, round)*. List these words on the *Plan-Do-Review Activity Worksheet* to serve as a reminder during the activity.

- Select Listening and Talking Tools to practice. List these strategies on the *Plan-Do-Review Activity Worksheet* to serve as a reminder during the activity.

- Gather a pillowcase and a variety of small objects (e.g., a brush, a spoon, a cotton ball, a cup, sandpaper, a ball, a shoe lace).

Do

- Talk to the child about what you will be doing together. Explain the sequence of events. For example, "We are going to play a guessing game. You will close your eyes. Then you will feel in the pillowcase. You will try to guess what you're touching. Then you can see if your guess was right."

- Place an item in the pillowcase while the child looks away. Have the child close his or her eyes and reach into the pillowcase to feel the object. Have him or her describe the item and guess its name. Then reveal the item. Continue with additional objects as long as the child is interested.

- Use Listening and Talking Tools when talking with the child as you play. For example:

  Use short, simple sentences—"Reach in the bag. Feel the object."

  Wait a few seconds before you reply to what the child says.

  Repeat the child's sentences and add to them—*"It is bumpy and big."*

Review

- Immediately after the activity, talk about what happened. For example, "Today we played a touch and feel game. First you felt a ball. Then you felt a cup. Last you felt a fork. You guessed all three." Complete a *Review Page*.

- Have the child draw a picture of the activity for a scrapbook page and write or tell a story about what happened. Encourage the child to show the picture or tell the story to another person (e.g., a sibling, a grandparent).

Extension Activities

- Play the Touch and Feel Game outside. Use items like rocks, leaves, and grass.
- Go to a pet store or local animal shelter and feel different animals.

Talk! Talk! Talk!

Vacuum Fun

Plan

- Select words you want the child to learn (e.g., *vacuum cleaner, dirty, under, behind, loud, dust*). List these words on the *Plan-Do-Review Activity Worksheet* to serve as a reminder during the activity.

- Select Listening and Talking Tools to practice. List these strategies on the *Plan-Do-Review Activity Worksheet* to serve as a reminder during the activity.

Do

- Talk to the child about what you will be doing together. Explain the sequence of events. For example, "We are going to vacuum the carpet. First let's vacuum the living room. Then we will vacuum the hall. Last we can vacuum the bedrooms."

- Have the child help you take out the vacuum cleaner, turn on the vacuum cleaner, and push the vacuum cleaner around to clean the carpets.

- Use Listening and Talking Tools when talking to the child as you vacuum together. For example:

  Talk about what you are doing—"I am plugging the cord into the outlet."

  Repeat the child's sentences and add to them—"Yes, *the carpet is dirty. We will clean it.*"

  Avoid interrupting the child—Wait for your child to finish talking before you turn on the vacuum.

Review

- Immediately after the activity, talk about what happened. For example, "Today we vacuumed the carpet. We used the vacuum cleaner to suck up the dust and dirt." Talk about what you vacuumed first, next, and last as you recall the activity with the child. Complete a *Review Page*.

- Have the child draw a picture of the activity for a scrapbook page and write or tell a story about what happened. Encourage the child to show the picture or tell the story to another person (e.g., a sibling, a grandparent).

Extension Activities
- Do other household chores with the child.
- Have the child help you vacuum the family car.

Color and Shape Collection

Plan

- Select words you want the child to learn (e.g., color words, shape words, *same, different, big, little*). List these words on the *Plan-Do-Review Activity Worksheet* to serve as a reminder during the activity.

- Select Listening and Talking Tools to practice. List these strategies on the *Plan-Do-Review Activity Worksheet* to serve as a reminder during the activity.

- Locate a storage container for the collection (e.g., a shoebox, a large plastic container).

Do

- Talk to the child about what you will be doing together. Explain the sequence of events. For example, "We are going to make a special collection. First we will decide what to collect. Then we will look in the yard and around the house for things to put in the collection. Last we will put the collection into a container."

- Let the child decide the theme for the collection (e.g., blue things, circles). Help the child search for items to add to the collection.

- Use Listening and Talking Tools when talking with the child as you locate items for the collection and place them in the storage container. For example:

  Show you are listening—Look at the child, nod your head, say "Uh-huh."

  Use new words—"This leaf is shaped like a *triangle.*"

  Model correct sentence forms—"The plate *is* round."

Review

- Immediately after the activity, talk about what happened. For example, "Today we made a collection of yellow things. We found lots of yellow leaves for the collection. The last thing we found was a yellow sticker. Our yellow collection is in a shoebox." Complete a *Review Page*.

- Have the child draw a picture of the activity for a scrapbook page and write or tell a story about what happened. Encourage the child to show the picture or the collection to another person (e.g., a sibling, a grandparent).

Extension Activities

- Read a story to the child about collecting things.
- Help the child separate toys into different groups.

Color Hunt

Plan

- Select words you want the child to learn (e.g., color words, *dark, light)*. List these words on the *Plan-Do-Review Activity Worksheet* to serve as a reminder during the activity.

- Select Listening and Talking Tools to practice. List these strategies on the *Plan-Do-Review Activity Worksheet* to serve as a reminder during the activity.

- Gather a pen or pencil and a piece of paper or writing tablet.

Do

- Talk to the child about what you will be doing together. Explain the sequence of events. For example, "We are going to play a game called Color Hunt. First we will go outside and look for yellow things. Then we will find blue things. Last we will find green things."

- Help the child hunt for objects of various colors. As you locate items, list them on the paper.

- Use Listening and Talking Tools when talking with the child as you hunt for colored objects. For example:

  Use short, simple sentences—"There is a flower. It is a yellow pansy."

  Talk about what you see—"I found a green dragonfly."

  Repeat new words often—"Here is a *blue* wagon and here is a *blue* ball."

Review

- Immediately after the activity, use the list you created and talk about what was found. For example, "Today we hunted for different colors. I found a yellow pansy. You found a green fire hydrant. We found lots of different colors." Talk about what you saw first, next, and last. Complete a *Review Page*.

- Have the child draw a picture of the activity for a scrapbook page and write or tell a story about what happened. Encourage the child to show the picture or tell the story to another person (e.g., a sibling, a grandparent).

Extension Activities
- During the Color Hunt, talk about light and dark shades of the various colors.
- Go on a Shape Hunt or a Size Hunt.

Foggy Shapes

Plan

- Select words you want the child to learn (e.g., shape words, *fog, mirror, steam, hot, circle, big, little)*. List these words on the *Plan-Do-Review Activity Worksheet* to serve as a reminder during the activity.

- Select Listening and Talking Tools to practice. List these strategies on the *Plan-Do-Review Activity Worksheet* to serve as a reminder during the activity.

Do

- Talk to the child about what you will be doing together. Explain the sequence of events. For example, "We are going to make shapes. First we will run hot water in the shower so that the bathroom mirror gets foggy. Then we will use our fingers to draw shapes on the foggy mirror."

- Go into the bathroom with the child and close the door. Run a hot shower for several minutes until the mirror is fogged. Draw various shapes on the mirror with the child.

- Use Listening and Talking Tools when talking with the child as you both draw shapes on the mirror. For example:

  Wait a few seconds before you reply to what the child says.

  Talk about what the child wants to talk about—"You want to draw circles? That sounds good."

  Avoid criticizing the child—"Good guess, but that's a triangle. That's a hard one to guess."

Review

- Immediately after the activity, talk about what happened. For example, "Today we had fun drawing shapes on a foggy mirror. The hot shower made the mirror foggy. Then we drew circles and squares on the mirror with our fingers." Complete a *Review Page*.

- Have the child draw a picture of the activity for a scrapbook page and write or tell a story about what happened. Encourage the child to show the picture or tell the story to another person (e.g., a sibling, a grandparent).

Extension Activities
- Draw letters and numbers on a foggy mirror.
- Use chalk to draw shapes on the driveway or sidewalk.

Magical Water

Plan

- Select words you want the child to learn (e.g., color words, *light, dark, change, same, different).* List these words on the *Plan-Do-Review Activity Worksheet* to serve as a reminder during the activity.

- Select Listening and Talking Tools to practice. List these strategies on the *Plan-Do-Review Activity Worksheet* to serve as a reminder during the activity.

- Gather several clear cups and several different colors of food coloring.

Do

- Talk to the child about what you will be doing together. Explain the sequence of events. For example, "We are going to have fun watching water change color. First we will fill the cups with water. Then we will put some food coloring in each cup to turn the water into a beautiful color. Last we can mix the colors together."

- Fill each cup about half-full of water. Help the child experiment by adding food coloring to the water. Help the child mix the various colors to make new colors (e.g., mix yellow and blue water to make green water).

- Use Listening and Talking Tools when talking with the child as you mix colors together. For example:

  Talk about what the child is doing—"You put two drops of red in the cup."

  Repeat the child's sentences and add to them—*"That is red.* It is dark red."

  Avoid changing topics quickly—Talk about one of the colors for several turns.

Review

- Immediately after the activity, talk about what happened. For example, "Today we had fun turning water into different colors. Then we had fun mixing colors together. It was like a magic trick." Complete a *Review Page.*

- Have the child draw a picture of the activity for a scrapbook page and write or tell a story about what happened. Encourage the child to show the picture or tell the story to another person (e.g., a sibling, a grandparent).

Extension Activities
- Use food coloring to make colored play dough.
- Use food coloring to color frosting. Then frost cookies or cupcakes.

Shape Cookies

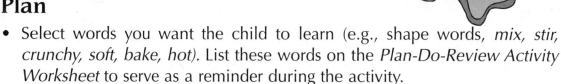

Plan

- Select words you want the child to learn (e.g., shape words, *mix, stir, crunchy, soft, bake, hot*). List these words on the *Plan-Do-Review Activity Worksheet* to serve as a reminder during the activity.

- Select Listening and Talking Tools to practice. List these strategies on the *Plan-Do-Review Activity Worksheet* to serve as a reminder during the activity.

- Gather the ingredients and utensils needed to make cut-out cookies. Find cookie cutters of several shapes.

Do

- Talk to the child about what you will be doing together. Explain the sequence of events. For example, "We are going to make cookies. First we will mix the ingredients. Then we will roll out the dough and cut out the cookies. We will bake the cookies in the oven. After the cookies cool, we will eat some."

- Make the shape cookies with the child. Have the child help with pouring ingredients, stirring, and cutting out shapes.

- Use Listening and Talking Tools when talking with the child as you make the cookies together. For example:

  Talk about what you see—"I see we have one egg left."

  Respond to the child's feelings—"It looks like you are having fun."

  Avoid criticizing the child—"Oops, you spilled some milk. That's okay."

Review

- Immediately after the activity, talk about what happened. For example, "Today we made cookies together. First we made circle cookies. Then we made square cookies. Now the cookies have cooled. Let's eat!" Complete a *Review Page*.

- Have the child draw a picture of the activity for a scrapbook page and write or tell a story about what happened. Encourage the child to show the picture or tell the story to another person (e.g., a sibling, a grandparent).

Extension Activities
- Talk about the different shapes of cookies you see at the grocery store.
- Talk about the textures of food as you eat them (e.g., soft, crunchy, chewy).

Cup Phone

Plan

- Select words you want the child to learn (e.g., *cup, string, knot*). List these words on the *Plan-Do-Review Activity Worksheet* to serve as a reminder during the activity.

- Select Listening and Talking Tools to practice. List these strategies on the *Plan-Do-Review Activity Worksheet* to serve as a reminder during the activity.

- Gather two Styrofoam cups, a piece of string about 10 feet long, and a pen.

Do

- Talk to the child about what you will be doing together. Explain the sequence of events. For example, "We are going to make a pretend telephone. First we are going to poke a little hole in the bottom of each cup. Then we will tie a long piece of string between the cups. Last we will talk to each other using the cup phone."

- Have the child help you make the cup phone. Using the pen, punch a small hole in the bottom of each cup. Insert one end of the string into each cup, through the bottoms. Tie a large knot on each end of the string (so the knots are inside the cups). Use the cup phone to exchange messages with the child.

- Use Listening and Talking Tools when using the cup phone with the child. For example:

  Wait a few seconds before you reply to what the child says.

  Repeat new words often—"I am tying a *knot*. It is a big *knot*. I tied a big *knot.*"

  Avoid interrupting the child—Wait for him or her to finish until you take your speaking turn.

Review

- Immediately after the activity, talk about what happened. For example, "Today we made a cup phone. First we tied the cups together with a piece of string. Then we talked on the phone for a long time." Complete a *Review Page*.

- Have the child draw a picture of the activity for a scrapbook page and write or tell a story about what happened. Encourage the child to show the picture or tell the story to another person (e.g., a sibling, a grandparent).

Extension Activities
- Visit a store and look at all the different types of telephones for sale.
- Go to a pay phone and show the child how it is used.

Dress-Up

Plan

- Select words you want the child to learn (e.g., names of body parts, names of clothing items, *purse, jewelry, mirror*). List these words on the *Plan-Do-Review Activity Worksheet* to serve as a reminder during the activity.

- Select Listening and Talking Tools to practice. List these strategies on the *Plan-Do-Review Activity Worksheet* to serve as a reminder during the activity.

- Gather clothing items, accessories, and a full-length mirror.

Do

- Talk to the child about what you will be doing together. Explain the sequence of events. For example, "We are going to play Dress-Up today. First we will put on clothes to wear when it is hot outside. Then we will put on clothes to wear when it is cold outside. We will use lots of different clothes."

- Have the child choose items to wear. Help the child with buttons, zippers, and accessory items.

- Use Listening and Talking Tools when talking with the child as you play Dress-Up together. For example:

  Talk about what the child is doing—"You are snapping your coat."

  Ask appropriate questions—"When do we need to wear boots?"

  Avoid interrupting the child.

Review

- Immediately after the activity, talk about what happened. For example, "Today we had so much fun playing Dress-Up. First you put on clothes for a snowy day. Then you put on summer clothes. We picked up all the clothes when we were done." Complete a *Review Page*.

- Have the child draw a picture of the activity for a scrapbook page and write or tell a story about what happened. Encourage the child to show the picture or tell the story to another person (e.g., a sibling, a grandparent).

Extension Activities

- Use doll clothes to dress up dolls and stuffed animals.
- Cut out pictures of clothing from magazines and catalogs. Talk about each item as you and the child glue the pictures onto construction paper.

Puppet Show

Plan

- Select words you want the child to learn (e.g., action words like *laugh, dance,* and *sing;* emotion words like *happy, scared,* and *surprised).* List these words on the *Plan-Do-Review Activity Worksheet* to serve as a reminder during the activity.

- Select Listening and Talking Tools to practice. List these strategies on the *Plan-Do-Review Activity Worksheet* to serve as a reminder during the activity.

- Gather a variety of materials to make two puppets (e.g., old socks, paper bags, markers, yarn, felt, glue, handkerchiefs).

Do

- Talk to the child about what you will be doing together. Explain the sequence of events. For example, "We are going to make two puppets. First we will draw eyes, a nose, and lips onto the socks. Then we will glue felt ears onto each puppet. Then we can play with the puppets."

- Have the child help you make two hand puppets. Use the markers to draw features onto old socks or paper bags. Consider cutting felt pieces and yarn for other features (e.g., hair, ears, clothing).

- Use Listening and Talking Tools when talking with the child as you create and play with the puppets. For example:

  Take only one speaking turn at a time—After your puppet says something, wait for the child to respond.

  Help the child by filling in difficult words—"That is called *yarn."*

  Avoid pressuring the child to talk—"It's okay if you don't want your puppet to sing. He can just dance."

Review

- Immediately after the activity, talk about what happened. For example, "Today we made sock puppets. First we made Simon. Then we made Frank. Simon and Frank danced together." Complete a *Review Page.*

- Have the child draw a picture of the activity for a scrapbook page and write or tell a story about the puppet. Encourage the child to show the picture or the puppet to another person (e.g., a sibling, a grandparent).

Extension Activities
• Use the puppets to retell familiar stories to each other.
• Go to a toy store and look at puppets with the child.

Talk! Talk! Talk!

Action Pics

Plan

- Select words you want the child to learn (e.g., action words like *walk, run, skip, eat, laugh;* pronouns like *he, she*). List these words on the *Plan-Do-Review Activity Worksheet* to serve as a reminder during the activity.

- Select Listening and Talking Tools to practice. List these strategies on the *Plan-Do-Review Activity Worksheet* to serve as a reminder during the activity.

- Gather a variety of pictures showing people involved in different actions (e.g., photographs or pictures from magazines).

Do

- Talk to the child about what you will be doing together. Explain the sequence of events. For example, "Let's look at pictures. We will see people doing things in the pictures. We can talk about what they are doing."

- Look through the pictures of people in action. Talk about what the person is doing in each picture.

- Use Listening and Talking Tools as you and the child talk about the action pictures. For example:

  Use new words—"He is *skipping.*"

  Model correct sentence forms—"He fell and skinned his knee."

  Avoid changing topics quickly—Talk about each picture for a little while before changing to a new picture.

Review

- Immediately after the activity, talk about what happened. For example, "Today we looked at lots of pictures. We talked about the pictures. First we saw a boy running and a man eating. Then we saw a baby crawling and a girl jumping." Complete a *Review Page.*

- Have the child draw a picture of the activity for a scrapbook page and write or tell a story about what happened. Encourage the child to show the picture or tell the story to another person (e.g., a sibling, a grandparent).

Extension Activities

- Take turns performing the actions that you see in the various pictures.
- Talk about actions that you and the child see during a television show or movie.

Action Rhyme Time

Plan

- Select words you want the child to learn (e.g., *up, down, clap, hop, jump*). List these words on the *Plan-Do-Review Activity Worksheet* to serve as a reminder during the activity.

- Select Listening and Talking Tools to practice. List these strategies on the *Plan-Do-Review Activity Worksheet* to serve as a reminder during the activity.

Do

- Talk to the child about what you will be doing together. Explain the sequence of events. For example, "We are going to sing some rhymes. We can do actions when we sing. First let's sing 'The Itsy-Bitsy Spider.' Then we can sing a different song."

- Perform a variety of action rhymes with the child. Refer to the words and actions provided on page 110.

- Use Listening and Talking Tools when talking with the child in between performing the action rhymes together. For example:

  Talk about what you did—"We clapped our hands really loud."

  Repeat the child's sentences and add to them—*"We had fun* singing and dancing!"

  Avoid pressuring the child to talk—"If you want, I'll sing first. You can sing it with me later."

Review

- Immediately after the activity, talk about what happened. For example, "Today we sang two action rhymes. First we did 'The Itsy-Bitsy Spider.' After that, we did 'If You're Happy and You Know It.' We had so much fun." Complete a *Review Page*.

- Have the child draw a picture of the activity for a scrapbook page and write or tell a story about what happened. Encourage the child to show the picture to or perform the action rhyme for another person (e.g., a sibling, a grandparent).

Extension Activities
- Visit the library or bookstore to find a book that has more action rhymes.
- Play children's audiotapes that contain various action songs and rhymes.

Familiar Action Rhymes

(Action words are in bold type.)

"If You're Happy and You Know It"

If you're happy and you know it, **clap** your hands (*clap, clap*).

If you're happy and you know it, **clap** your hands (*clap, clap*).

If you're happy and you know it, then your face will surely show it.

If you're happy and you know it, **clap** your hands (*clap, clap*).

*(Repeat the song with various actions such as
"**tap** your head" and "**hop** around.")*

"The Itsy-Bitsy Spider"

The itsy-bitsy spider **climbed** up the water spout.
(Move your index fingers and thumbs in an upward chain.)

Down **came** the rain and **washed** the spider out.
*(Move your fingers in a downward motion for rain.
Cross and uncross your arms quickly to "wash the spider out.")*

Out **came** the sun and **dried up** all the rain.
(Make a big circle overhead with your arms for the sun.)

And the itsy-bitsy spider **climbed** up the spout again.
(Move your index fingers and thumbs in an upward chain.)

"Open Shut Them"

*(Gesture with your hands as indicated.
Have the child try to imitate your gestures.)*

Open shut them, **open shut** them, **give** a little **clap.**

Open shut them, **open shut** them, **put** them in your lap.

Creep them, **crawl** them, **creep** them, **crawl** them, right up to your chin.

Open wide your little mouth, but do not let them in.

"Teddy Bear, Teddy Bear"

Teddy Bear, Teddy Bear, **turn** around (*spin around*).

Teddy Bear, Teddy Bear, **touch** the ground (*touch the ground with your hands*).

Teddy Bear, Teddy Bear, **tap** your shoe (*tap your toe on the ground*).

Teddy Bear, Teddy Bear, that will do.

Talk! Talk! Talk!

Simon Says

Plan

- Select words you want the child to learn (e.g., body parts; action words such as *jump, wave, open, hop, bend)*. List these words on the *Plan-Do-Review Activity Worksheet* to serve as a reminder during the activity.

- Select Listening and Talking Tools to practice. List these strategies on the *Plan-Do-Review Activity Worksheet* to serve as a reminder during the activity.

Do

- Talk to the child about what you will be doing together. Explain the sequence of events. For example, "We are going to play a game called Simon Says. First I will be Simon. I will tell you things to do. Then you can be Simon. You will tell me things to do."

- For younger children, take turns giving and receiving action directions with the child. Start each direction with the phrase "Simon says" (e.g., "Simon says bend your arm"). For older children, tell them to only respond to directions that begin with the phrase "Simon says." In these cases, vary which directions begin with "Simon says."

- Use Listening and Talking Tools when talking with the child as you play Simon Says together. For example:

  Look at the child in the face (while giving and receiving directions).

  Talk about what you are doing—"Simon said jump. I am jumping."

  Model correct sentence forms—"Oh! I should kneel *on the ground*. I see."

Review

- Immediately after the activity, talk about what happened. For example, "Today we played Simon Says. First I was Simon. Then you were Simon. We had fun doing all sorts of actions." Complete a *Review Page*.

- Have the child draw a picture of the activity for a scrapbook page and write or tell a story about what happened. Encourage the child to show the picture or tell the story to another person (e.g., a sibling, a grandparent).

Extension Activities

- Play the game Follow the Leader with the child.
- Perform actions in front of a full-length mirror with the child.

Playground Fun

Plan

- Select words you want the child to learn (e.g., *top, under, across, high, low, up, down, fast, slow)*. List these words on the *Plan-Do-Review Activity Worksheet* to serve as a reminder during the activity.

- Select Listening and Talking Tools to practice. List these strategies on the *Plan-Do-Review Activity Worksheet* to serve as a reminder during the activity.

Do

- Talk to the child about what you will be doing together. Explain the sequence of events. For example, "We are going to go to the playground. We can use the slide, the monkey bars, and the swings. We can play in the sandbox too."

- Take the child to a playground and play with him or her on the equipment.

- Use Listening and Talking Tools when talking with the child as you play together. For example:

    Talk about what you see—"There are two kids in the sandbox."

    Use new words—"You are crawling *through* the tunnel."

    Avoid pressuring the child to talk—"You can use the swing now. Maybe later we can talk about what you like best on the playground."

Review

- Immediately after the activity, talk about what happened. For example, "Today we went to the park. We played on the toys at the playground. First we played on the slide. Then we played on the swings. Last we played in the sand." Complete a *Review Page*.

- Have the child draw a picture of the activity for a scrapbook page and write or tell a story about what happened. Encourage the child to show the picture or tell the story to another person (e.g., a sibling, a grandparent).

Extension Activities
- Use straws or popsicle sticks to build model playground structures.
- Take the child to an indoor playground at a local fast-food restaurant.

Talk! Talk! Talk!

Shadow Time

Plan

- Select words you want the child to learn (e.g., *shadow, dark, light, same, different*). List these words on the *Plan-Do-Review Activity Worksheet* to serve as a reminder during the activity.

- Select Listening and Talking Tools to practice. List these strategies on the *Plan-Do-Review Activity Worksheet* to serve as a reminder during the activity.

Do

- Talk to the child about what you will be doing together. Explain the sequence of events. For example, "It is a sunny day. We are going to make shadows outside. First we will go outside. We will stand in the sunshine to make shadows."

- Take turns making shadows with the child using various body and hand shapes (e.g., a butterfly, a circle, an X, a thumbs-up signal, a T, a ball).

- Use Listening and Talking Tools when talking with the child as you make shadows together. For example:

  Show you are listening—Nod your head and look at the child in the face when he or she is talking.

  Talk about what the child is doing—"You are making a circle."

  Model correct sentence forms—"It *is* a butterfly."

Review

- Immediately after the activity, talk about what happened. For example, "Today we made shadows outside. We went out in the yard and made lots of shapes. You made a circle with your arms. I made an X with my arms and legs." Complete a *Review Page*.

- Have the child draw a picture of the activity for a scrapbook page and write or tell a story about what happened. Encourage the child to show the picture or tell the story to another person (e.g., a sibling, a grandparent).

Extension Activities
- Go outside at night and talk about the moonlight.
- In a darkened room, set stuffed animals or other toys in front of a flashlight to make shadows.

Talk! Talk! Talk!

Sink or Float?

Plan

- Select words you want the child to learn (e.g., *float, floating, floated, sink, sinking, sunk, heavy, light*). List these words on the *Plan-Do-Review Activity Worksheet* to serve as a reminder during the activity.

- Select Listening and Talking Tools to practice. List these strategies on the *Plan-Do-Review Activity Worksheet* to serve as a reminder during the activity.

- Locate a large tub and five or more objects to set in the water.

Do

- Talk to the child about what you will be doing together. Explain the sequence of events. For example, "We are going to play a game called Sink or Float? today. We are going to go outside and fill a tub with water. Then we are going to set things in the water. We will see what sinks and what floats."

- Go outside and have the child help you fill the tub with water. Have the child locate items to set in the water. Have the child set various items in the water to see if each sinks or floats. If possible, have the child take a guess whether the item will sink or float before setting each in water.

- Use Listening and Talking Tools when talking with the child as you experiment with the objects in the water. For example:

  Wait a few seconds before you reply to what the child says.

  Talk about what you see—"The rock sank. It went down fast."

  Respond to the child's feelings—"Are you surprised that the leaf floated?"

Review

- Immediately after the activity, talk about what happened. For example, "Today we played the Sink or Float? game. First we saw the cork float. Then we saw the rock sink. Last we saw a marble sink." Complete a *Review Page*.

- Have the child draw a picture of the activity for a scrapbook page and write or tell a story about what happened. Encourage the child to show the picture or tell the story to another person (e.g., a sibling, a grandparent).

Extension Activities

- After testing each object in the water, start one pile for items that sank and one pile for items that floated.
- Play the Sink or Float? game when washing dishes with the child.

Tall and Short Things

Plan

- Select words you want the child to learn (e.g., *tall, taller, tallest, short, shorter, shortest*). List these words on the *Plan-Do-Review Activity Worksheet* to serve as a reminder during the activity.

- Select Listening and Talking Tools to practice. List these strategies on the *Plan-Do-Review Activity Worksheet* to serve as a reminder during the activity.

Do

- Talk to the child about what you will be doing together. Explain the sequence of events. For example, "We are going to find tall things and short things. First we will look outside. Then we will look inside."

- Help the child look for tall objects and short objects.

- Use Listening and Talking Tools when talking with the child as you walk along together. For example:

  Talk about what you see—"The tree is taller than the swing set."

  Repeat the child's sentences and add to them—*"The ladder is tall* and red."

  Avoid criticizing the child—"You are right. That tree is tall, but the white one is the tallest."

Review

- Immediately after the activity, talk about what happened. For example, "Today we went for a walk and looked for short things and tall things. The telephone pole was the tallest thing we saw. The curb was the shortest thing we saw." Complete a *Review Page*.

- Have the child draw a picture of the activity for a scrapbook page and write or tell a story about what happened. Encourage the child to show the picture or tell the story to another person (e.g., a sibling, a grandparent).

Extension Activities
- Help the child draw a picture of his or her family members standing in line from shortest to tallest.
- Help the child arrange sticks in line from shortest to tallest.

Talk! Talk! Talk!

Up and Down Game

Plan

- Select words you want the child to learn (e.g., *up, down, high, low, near, far, above, below, around).* List these words on the *Plan-Do-Review Activity Worksheet* to serve as a reminder during the activity.

- Select Listening and Talking Tools to practice. List these strategies on the *Plan-Do-Review Activity Worksheet* to serve as a reminder during the activity.

Do

- Talk to the child about what you will be doing together. Explain the sequence of events. For example, "Let's go outside and play a game called Up and Down. First we will look up and tell what we see. Then we will look down and tell what we see. We can walk around while we are looking up and looking down."

- Take the child outside and look up and down as you walk around and talk about what you see.

- Use Listening and Talking Tools when talking with the child as you walk along together looking for objects. For example:

  Talk about what you see—"I looked up and saw a bird."

  Talk about what you are doing—"I am looking down at the ground."

  Talk about what the child wants to talk about—"You think we should look up? What do you see?"

Review

- Immediately after the activity, talk about what happened. For example, "Today we played a game called Up and Down. First we looked up and saw a bird, two clouds, and an airplane. Then we looked down and saw the grass, a flower, and some ants." Complete a *Review Page.*

- Have the child draw a picture of the activity for a scrapbook page and write or tell a story about what happened. Encourage the child to show the picture or tell the story to another person (e.g., a sibling, a grandparent).

Extension Activities
- Play the Up and Down Game indoors.
- Play on a teeter-totter with the child and talk about who is up and who is down.

Bug Collection

Plan

- Select words you want the child to learn (e.g., *bug, insect, wings, stinger, web, fly, crawl, creep, buzz*). List these words on the *Plan-Do-Review Activity Worksheet* to serve as a reminder during the activity.

- Select Listening and Talking Tools to practice. List these strategies on the *Plan-Do-Review Activity Worksheet* to serve as a reminder during the activity.

- Locate at least one jar with a lid. Punch several holes in the lid.

Do

- Talk to the child about what you will be doing together. Explain the sequence of events. For example, "We are going to catch bugs today. First we will put some leaves and grass inside a jar. Then we will look for different bugs on plants, trees, and rocks. We can put the bugs in the jar."

- Take the child outside to look for bugs. Have the child put some grass and a few leaves in the jar. Locate and place interesting bugs in the jar.

- Use Listening and Talking Tools when talking with the child as you observe and catch bugs together. For example:

  Look at the child in the face (while giving and receiving directions).

  Repeat part or all of the child's sentences in question form—"That *bug is pretty?*"

  Model correct sentence forms—"That *is* a caterpillar."

Review

- Immediately after the activity, talk about what happened. For example, "Today we collected bugs. First we found a caterpillar. Then we found a ladybug. The caterpillar was long and the ladybug was round." Complete a *Review Page*.

- Have the child draw a picture of the activity for a scrapbook page and write or tell a story about what happened. Encourage the child to show the picture or tell the story to another person (e.g., a sibling, a grandparent).

Extension Activities
- Use a variety of craft materials (e.g., pipe cleaners, beads) to make bugs.
- Perform various bug actions with the child (e.g., crawling, climbing, spinning, wriggling, flying).

Flower Fun

Plan

- Select words you want the child to learn (e.g., *petal, stem, leaf,* color words). List these words on the *Plan-Do-Review Activity Worksheet* to serve as a reminder during the activity.

- Select Listening and Talking Tools to practice. List these strategies on the *Plan-Do-Review Activity Worksheet* to serve as a reminder during the activity.

- Gather a sheet of white construction paper, several pieces of colored construction paper, a pencil, scissors, and glue.

Do

- Talk to the child about what you will be doing together. Explain the sequence of events. For example, "We are going to make beautiful flowers. We will use colored paper to make the petals, stems, and leaves. We will cut out the pieces and glue them onto a big sheet of paper."

- Help the child draw flower petals, stems, and leaves on the construction paper (use real flower petals and leaves as a pattern, if desired). Help the child cut out the pieces and glue them onto the large sheet of white construction paper.

- Use Listening and Talking Tools when talking with the child as you create the paper flowers together. For example:

  Take only one speaking turn at a time.

  Repeat new words often—"This *petal* is red. This *petal* is round."

  Ask appropriate questions—"What color should we use?"

Review

- Immediately after the activity, talk about what happened. For example, "Today we made flowers. First we drew the pieces. Then we cut out the pieces. Last we glued the flowers onto white paper." Complete a *Review Page*.

- Have the child draw a picture of the activity for a scrapbook page and write or tell a story about what happened. Encourage the child to show the picture or tell the story to another person (e.g., a sibling, a grandparent).

Extension Activities

- Help the child pick flowers and arrange them in a vase.
- Make a dandelion chain necklace with the child.

Talk! Talk! Talk!

Paper-Bag Mask

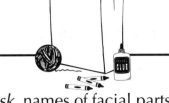

Plan

- Select words you want the child to learn (e.g., *mask,* names of facial parts, names of craft supplies). List these words on the *Plan-Do-Review Activity Worksheet* to serve as a reminder during the activity.

- Select Listening and Talking Tools to practice. List these strategies on the *Plan-Do-Review Activity Worksheet* to serve as a reminder during the activity.

- Gather a large paper grocery bag, glue, markers, scissors, and a variety of craft supplies (e.g., cotton balls, yarn, feathers, buttons, construction paper).

Do

- Talk to the child about what you will be doing together. Explain the sequence of events. For example, "We are going to make a mask. First we will choose things to use for hair, eyes, a nose, a mouth, and ears. Then we will glue all the pieces onto the mask. When it's done, you can wear the mask."

- Have the child choose different craft supplies to use for the mask. Help the child glue the items onto the paper bag. After the mask has dried, let the child wear the mask.

- Use Listening and Talking Tools when talking with the child as you make the mask together. For example:

  Wait a few seconds before you reply to what the child says.

  Help the child by filling in difficult words—"That's called a *button."*

  Avoid pressuring the child to talk—"We can talk about the mask later."

Review

- Immediately after the activity, talk about what happened. For example, "Today we made a mask. We used buttons for the eyes and nose. We glued feathers on for hair. We used markers to draw the mouth." Complete a *Review Page.*

- Have the child draw a picture of the activity for a scrapbook page and write or tell a story about what happened. Encourage the child to show the picture or tell the story to another person (e.g., a sibling, a grandparent).

Extension Activities

- Have the child wear the mask while telling a story or singing a song.
- Use face paint to paint a design on the child's cheeks.

Pumpkin Carving

Plan

- Select words you want the child to learn (e.g., *pumpkin, scooping, seeds, scary, inside,* names of facial parts). List these words on the *Plan-Do-Review Activity Worksheet* to serve as a reminder during the activity.

- Select Listening and Talking Tools to practice. List these strategies on the *Plan-Do-Review Activity Worksheet* to serve as a reminder during the activity.

- Gather a pumpkin, a large knife, a large spoon, several sheets of old newspaper or paper towels, and a black marker or pen.

Do

- Talk to the child about what you will be doing together. Explain the sequence of events. For example, "We are going to carve a pumpkin. First we will draw a face on the pumpkin. Then we will cut off the top and scoop out the seeds. Last we will cut out the face parts."

- Set the pumpkin on the newspaper or paper towels. Have the child help draw a face on the pumpkin. Cut off the top of the pumpkin and have the child help scoop out the seeds. Then cut out the face parts.

- Use Listening and Talking Tools when talking with the child as you work on the pumpkin together. For example:

  Use new words—"The pumpkin is *orange."*

  Repeat new words often—"I am cutting an *eye.* The *eye* is a triangle."

  Avoid criticizing the child—"We could put the nose in the middle instead of on the bottom."

Review

- Immediately after the activity, talk about what happened. For example, "Today we carved a pumpkin. We scooped out the seeds that were inside. The pumpkin has two eyes, a nose, and a mouth." Complete a *Review Page.*

- Have the child draw a picture of the activity for a scrapbook page and write or tell a story about what happened. Encourage the child to show the picture or tell the story to another person (e.g., a sibling, a grandparent).

Extension Activities
- Read the child a story about pumpkins or Halloween.
- Help the child roast or plant the pumpkin seeds.

Season Bag

Plan

- Select words you want the child to learn (e.g., seasonal words such as *flower* and *umbrella* for spring; *swimsuit* and *sunglasses* for summer; *leaf* and *pumpkin* for fall; *mitten* and *scarf* for winter). List these words on the *Plan-Do-Review Activity Worksheet* to serve as a reminder during the activity.

- Select Listening and Talking Tools to practice. List these strategies on the *Plan-Do-Review Activity Worksheet* to serve as a reminder during the activity.

- Gather a pillowcase or a paper bag and an array of seasonal objects.

Do

- Talk to the child about what you will be doing together. Explain the sequence of events. For example, "We are going to play a guessing game. You will close your eyes, and I will put something in the bag. Then you can reach into the bag and try to guess what's inside. After you guess, you can look at the object."

- Place an item in the bag while the child looks away. Have the child reach into the bag, touch the object, and guess its name. Give the child clues if needed. Then have him or her remove the item from the bag. Continue with additional items as long as the child remains interested.

- Use Listening and Talking Tools when talking with the child as you play the game together. For example:

  Take only one speaking turn at a time.

  Repeat the child's sentences and add to them—*"It's a brown mitten."*

  Avoid interrupting the child.

Review

- Immediately after the activity, talk about what happened. For example, "First you found a flower in the season bag. Then you found your swimsuit in the bag. Last you found a scarf." Complete a *Review Page*.

- Have the child draw a picture of the activity for a scrapbook page and write or tell a story about what happened. Encourage the child to show the picture or tell the story to another person (e.g., a sibling, a grandparent).

Extension Activities

- Read seasonal stories to the child.
- Have the child choose an object to put in the bag for you to feel and guess.

Snow Person

Plan

- Select words you want the child to learn (e.g., *top, middle, bottom, little, medium, big, melting*). List these words on the *Plan-Do-Review Activity Worksheet* to serve as a reminder during the activity.

- Select Listening and Talking Tools to practice. List these strategies on the *Plan-Do-Review Activity Worksheet* to serve as a reminder during the activity.

Do

- Talk to the child about what you will be doing together. Explain the sequence of events. For example, "We are going to go outside and make a snow person today. First we will roll a big snowball for the bottom. Then we will make medium snowball for the middle. Then we will make a small snowball for the top. Last we will use rocks and sticks to add a face and arms to the snow person."

- Go outside and build a snow person with the child.

- Use Listening and Talking Tools when talking with the child as you build a snow person together. For example:

  Talk about what you are doing—"I am rolling the smallest snowball."

  Ask appropriate questions—"Where does this snowball go?"

  Avoid interrupting the child.

Review

- Immediately after the activity, talk about what happened. For example, "Today we went outside and built a snow person. First we rolled a huge snowball. Then we rolled a medium-sized snowball. Next we made a small snowball for the head. Last we used rocks to make the face." Complete a *Review Page*.

- Have the child draw a picture of the activity for a scrapbook page and write or tell a story about what happened. Encourage the child to show the picture or tell the story to another person (e.g., a sibling, a grandparent).

Extension Activities
- Read the child a story about wintertime.
- Use black construction paper and white crayons to draw snow people together.

Bus Ride

Plan

- Select words you want the child to learn (e.g., *bus, wheels, window, bell, seat, driver, token)*. List these words on the *Plan-Do-Review Activity Worksheet* to serve as a reminder during the activity.

- Select Listening and Talking Tools to practice. List these strategies on the *Plan-Do-Review Activity Worksheet* to serve as a reminder during the activity.

Do

- Talk to the child about what you will be doing together. Explain the sequence of events. For example, "We are going to take a bus ride today. First we are going to walk to the bus stop. Then we are going to wait for the bus. We will ride the bus to the library."

- Take a ride on a bus with the child. Have the child help pay the fare and ring the bell.

- Use Listening and Talking Tools when talking with the child as you ride the bus together. For example:

  Repeat the child's sentences and add to them—*"The bus is big and blue."*

  Model correct sentence forms—"We used two token*s.*"

  Avoid pressuring the child to talk—"If you want to, you can say 'Hi' to the bus driver."

Review

- Immediately after the activity, talk about what happened. For example, "Today we took a bus ride. We waited for the bus. We rode the bus to the library. Then we rode the bus back. The bus was very big. We had fun." Complete a *Review Page*.

- Have the child draw a picture of the activity for a scrapbook page and write or tell a story about what happened. Encourage the child to show the picture or tell the story to another person (e.g., a sibling, a grandparent).

Extension Activities

- Read the child a story about riding a bus.
- Use a cardboard box to make a play bus for the child.

Car Time

Plan

- Select words you want the child to learn (e.g., color words, letter names, vehicle names, animal names). List these words on the *Plan-Do-Review Activity Worksheet* to serve as a reminder during the activity.

- Select Listening and Talking Tools to practice. List these strategies on the *Plan-Do-Review Activity Worksheet* to serve as a reminder during the activity.

Do

- Talk to the child about what you will be doing together. Explain the sequence of events. For example, "We are going to go for a car ride. While we are riding in the car, we will talk about the colors we see. Maybe we can look for red things and green things. We can also look for letters. Let's find the letters A, B, and C."

- While riding in the car with the child, talk about the colors, letters, and other things the two of you see.

- Use Listening and Talking Tools when talking with the child as you ride in the car. For example:

  Take only one speaking turn at a time—"I see a blue car. What do you see?"

  Ask appropriate questions—"What color is the bus you see?"

  Avoid interrupting the child.

Review

- Immediately after the activity, talk about what happened. For example, "Today we went for a long car ride. We saw lots of blue things, like the sky, a car, and a house. We saw lots of animals too. We saw a horse, a cow, and three dogs." Complete a *Review Page*.

- Have the child draw a picture of the activity for a scrapbook page and write or tell a story about what happened. Encourage the child to show the picture or tell the story to another person (e.g., a sibling, a grandparent).

Extension Activities
• Play with the child using small toy cars.
• Have the child help you wash the car.

Vehicle Search

Plan

- Select words you want the child to learn (e.g., *van, car, truck, motorcycle, bus, taxi, fire truck, police car, train*). List these words on the *Plan-Do-Review Activity Worksheet* to serve as a reminder during the activity.

- Select Listening and Talking Tools to practice. List these strategies on the *Plan-Do-Review Activity Worksheet* to serve as a reminder during the activity.

- Gather drawing paper and crayons.

Do

- Talk to the child about what you will be doing together. Explain the sequence of events. For example, "We are going to take a walk and look for all sorts of vehicles. We might see cars, trucks, motorcycles, and trains. When we are done with our walk, we can draw pictures of the vehicles we found."

- Take a walk with the child and search for vehicles. After the walk, draw pictures of the vehicles you found.

- Use Listening and Talking Tools when talking with the child as you walk together and look for vehicles. For example:

  Show you are listening—Look at the child, nod your head, and say things like "Um-hmm" and "I see."

  Repeat new words often—"The *train* is long. The *train* is big."

  Avoid criticizing the child—"That looks like a bicycle, but it's really a motorcycle. You don't need to pedal it."

Review

- Immediately after the activity, talk about what happened. For example, "Today we went for a walk and searched for vehicles. We found lots of cars. We saw two big trucks. Last we saw a green bus. When we were done, we drew pictures of the vehicles." Complete a *Review Page*.

- Have the child draw a picture of the activity for a scrapbook page and write or tell a story about what happened. Encourage the child to show the picture or tell the story to another person (e.g., a sibling, a grandparent).

Extension Activities
- Visit a car dealership with the child.
- Read stories to the child about different vehicles.

Appendices

Listening and Talking Tools Report Card

The *Listening and Talking Tools Report Card* includes a listing of 24 of the 25 strategies presented in Chapter 1 (all the Listening and Talking Tools except number 1—"Children will listen carefully if they can hear adequately"). In addition, the days of the week are listed across the top of the page. This can be a useful tool to help adults monitor their own use of the Listening and Talking Tools on a daily basis. Duplicate the report card and distribute it to the adult learners whenever necessary. Start using this form with the adult learners even before you have introduced all the tools. Have the adults use a highlighting marker to keep track of the strategies they have learned. Consider reviewing completed report cards with the adults whenever possible.

Listening and Talking Tools Report Card

Directions: Use this report card to keep track of the strategies you are using during your interactions with a child. Highlight the Listening and Talking Tools you are practicing. After conducting an activity with a child, go through the list of highlighted strategies and indicate with a check (✓) when you feel you used a strategy successfully during the activity.

Listening and Talking Tools	Sunday	Monday	Tuesday	Wednesday	Thursday	Friday	Saturday
Talk more slowly.							
Get the child's attention before you talk.							
Make sure that it is quiet.							
Use short, simple sentences.							
Look at the child in the face.							
Wait a few seconds before replying.							
Take one speaking turn at a time.							
Show you are listening.							
Talk about what you are doing.							
Talk about what the child is doing.							
Talk about what the child wants to talk about.							
Talk about what you see.							
Use new words.							
Repeat new words often.							
Repeat part or all of the child's sentences in question form.							
Repeat the child's sentences and add to them.							
Help the child start a sentence or fill in difficult words.							
Model correct sentence forms.							
Respond to the child's feelings.							
Ask appropriate questions.							
Avoid criticizing the child.							
Avoid pressuring the child to talk.							
Avoid interrupting the child.							
Avoid changing topics quickly.							

Talk! Talk! Talk!

Review Page

WHAT I did:

_____

_____

_____

_____

_____

WHO I did it with:

_____

WORDS I learned:

_____

_____

Here is my picture or photo and story about what I did:

Please return this form to _____ *by* _____.

Calendar Activities

This appendix includes calendars that provide caregivers with an array of activities for practicing their Listening and Talking Tools with their children. Prior to presenting the first calendar, distribute a copy of page 133 to each adult. This page acquaints adults with the purpose and use of the activity calendars. At the beginning of each month, distribute one activity calendar to adults. As needed, demonstrate calendar activities to the adults before sending each calendar home. Encourage adults to use the Plan-Do-Review format when conducting each day's activity. As an option, distribute copies of the *Plan-Do-Review Activity Worksheet* (page 86) for adults to use to outline select calendar activities. Distribute and encourage adults to use *Review Pages* (page 131) during the review stage of some calendar activities.

Some calendar activities may be used during intervention sessions with children as a "warm-up" activity at the beginning of the session or as a transition activity when moving from one task to another. Be creative when using the activities described on the calendars.

Calendar Activities
Suggestions for Caregivers

It is important to take time to do activities with your child every day. At the beginning of each month, you will receive an activity calendar. These calendars provide ways to practice the Listening and Talking Tools you learn. The calendars contain fun and simple activities that will help you expose your child to appropriate vocabulary and concepts every day of the month. The activities require very little planning and can be easily completed in and around the home.

When you receive a calendar, number the days. Complete an activity with your child every day. Follow the daily suggestion or choose to repeat an activity if the daily selection is not appropriate for your circumstances. Turn each activity into a language lesson as you model, expand, and extend the interactions that occur between you and your child.

Have fun with these activities. Always remember to Talk! Talk! Talk!

January

Sunday	Monday	Tuesday	Wednesday	Thursday	Friday	Saturday
Look at this month's calendar and talk about the important dates. Draw a circle around those dates.	Make footprints in the snow, grass, or sand. Talk about their shapes and sizes.	Talk about some activities you might do if it snows (e.g. sledding, skating, making a snow person).	Cut pictures from a magazine and make a collage with glue and construction paper.	Use a marker to draw a face on an old sock. Use the sock as a hand puppet.	Use food coloring at dinner to turn potatoes green. Talk about how potatoes grow.	Make the bed. Talk about how the pillows and mattress are rectangles.
Fold clothes together. Separate the items into piles.	Sing an action song such as *The Itsy-Bitsy Spider.*	Draw a picture and use words like *tall, short, fat,* and *skinny* when drawing.	Name baby animals (e.g., *puppy, kitten, lamb, calf, cub,* and *chick*). Describe what each animal looks like.	Do actions (e.g., *hop, skip, roll,* and *slide*) and talk about what you are doing.	Choose an animal and talk about what it looks like, what it eats, and where it lives.	Use watered-down dish detergent to blow bubbles. Talk about how bubbles move.
Find a short poem and recite it often.	Match a pile of mittens or socks.	Read a winter story.	Talk about the different jobs people have.	Make popcorn and change its color by adding food coloring. Talk about how popcorn pops.	Shovel the snow on the sidewalk or clear twigs from the lawn. Talk about what you are doing.	Make a picnic lunch to eat in the living room or in the backyard.
Act out a favorite story, such as *Goldilocks and the Three Bears.*	Cut out the initials of your child's name from a large piece of paper. Hang them on the refrigerator door.	Roll a ball into a pail that has been laid on its side. Talk about how the ball rolls.	Set up an obstacle course in a room. Talk about climbing *under, over, inside,* and *between.*	Talk about things in a room that are round.	Name an adjective, such as *shiny,* and then name things that the word describes (e.g., mirror, car, spoon).	Draw flowers on paper and tape them all over a room.
Place a carnation in food coloring and water. Watch the flower change color.	Play Store with the canned goods in your kitchen.	Make a poster of smiley faces to put on the refrigerator. Show the poster to guests.	Draw a thermometer and describe what happens when the weather is very cold or very hot.	Draw how the weather looks outside and use words to describe it, such as *cold, windy,* and *sunny.*	Look at a photograph of family members. Name everyone and talk about what is happening in the picture.	Look back at this month's calendar, and talk about the important things that happened.

Talk! Talk! Talk!

February

Sunday	Monday	Tuesday	Wednesday	Thursday	Friday	Saturday
Look at this month's calendar and talk about the important dates. Draw a circle around those dates.	Read a book about groundhogs.	Find things in the house that feel furry like a groundhog.	Make pancakes. Put fruit on top. Describe the fruit.	Recite a simple poem like "Humpty Dumpty" or "Little Jack Horner."	Make pudding. Talk about the thin milk and the thick pudding.	Fill the kitchen sink with water. Play in the water with a variety of containers.
Take giant steps down the hall or on the sidewalk. Count your steps.	Sort the knives, spoons, and forks in the kitchen silverware drawer.	Count while you make big and little circles with your arms.	Draw a big heart on paper. Color it red.	Talk about all the people you love.	Look for all the red things in a room.	Bake cookies and put cinnamon hearts on them.
Place your hand under running water and see the splashes it makes. Talk about whether the water is warm, hot, or cold.	Make shapes, letters, and numbers with your fingers.	Fold and tear paper napkins into different shapes.	Make a picture with lots of lines and hang it on a bedroom door.	Take turns standing on a scale and talk about who is heavier and who is lighter.	Locate small and large chairs in the house.	Look for things in the house that have stripes.
Draw thick lines and thin lines on paper and hang the paper in the window so that the sun shines through it.	Cut an apple into quarters. Count all the seeds.	Look at a magazine and cut out pictures of people in action (e.g., eating, swimming, running, driving a car).	Wear red clothes today. Talk about light and dark shades of red.	Put all the gloves and mittens in pairs.	Talk about what makes you laugh.	Practice whispering. Talk about when it's appropriate to whisper.
Take the lamp shade off a lamp, turn on the light bulb, and make shadows on the wall with your fingers.	Look at the moon. Talk about its shape, color, and size.	Jump around the living room. Count the number of jumps.	Put all the shoes, slippers, and boots in pairs.	Talk about what makes you feel happy.	Look at a photo of relatives. Talk about who they are and where they live.	Look back at this month's calendar, and talk about the important things that happened.

Talk! Talk! Talk!

March

Sunday	Monday	Tuesday	Wednesday	Thursday	Friday	Saturday
Look at this month's calendar and talk about the important dates. Draw a circle around those dates.	Talk about all the green things in a room.	Watch a favorite TV show and talk about it.	Sweep the kitchen floor. Use new words like *broom, dustpan,* and *dirt.*	Make a cake and frost it with a special color of frosting.	Read a story, such as *Little Red Riding Hood,* and draw a picture of the main character.	Count all the clocks in the house.
Talk about bugs you see outside and where they live.	Find items in the basement or garage that are shaped like a triangle.	Name animals and make the sounds they make.	Make a telephone call.	Organize the toy box.	Play a card game. Talk about the rules.	Trace hands and feet on paper. Decorate them with craft supplies.
Cut out pictures of fruit from a magazine. Glue them onto a large piece of paper.	Hop down the hall or across the room. Count the number of hops.	Use a flashlight to search in a closet. Talk about what you find.	Color a picture and talk about the colors.	Look at a brush and a comb. Talk about how they are the same and how they are different.	Touch things in the room and describe how they feel.	Fill glasses with different levels of water, and listen to the sounds as you tap the glasses with a spoon.
Cut out pink and blue things from a magazine. Make a collage.	Sing with a favorite audiotape.	Look at a store advertisement and find different numbers.	Make a milkshake and talk about all the different ingredients.	Visit the airport and watch the planes take off and land.	Go for a walk and look for white cars.	Make a spaceship from a cardboard box. Tell a story about space travel.
Pretend to be different storybook characters. Act like the characters.	Draw funny faces on a steamy mirror.	Dance to music and talk about your actions.	Find the biggest and smallest stuffed animal in the house.	Look at a photograph and draw a picture of it.	Listen to the noises outside. Try to guess what they might be.	Look back at this month's calendar, and talk about the important things that happened.

Talk! Talk! Talk!

April

Sunday	Monday	Tuesday	Wednesday	Thursday	Friday	Saturday
Look at this month's calendar and talk about the important dates. Draw a circle around those dates.	Make a fancy sandwich by cutting the crusts off or by cutting it into different shapes.	Talk about animals people have as pets (e.g., dogs, cats, birds, and hamsters).	Look outside and find things that are brown.	Find rectangles in the kitchen.	Make a tent using a sheet and furniture. Pretend to go camping.	Stretch to be tall, narrow, and long. Scrunch down to be short, wide, and small.
Take turns scooping sand with your hands and filling up a bucket.	Clean the bathtub using a variety of scrubbing motions (e.g., circular, zigzag).	Make ice cubes using fruit juice instead of water.	Talk about words that rhyme with *cat*.	Name your relatives and talk about where they live.	Draw a picture of your house.	Count all the doors in the house.
Go to a store and buy fruit. Talk about all the different fruits.	Write with colored pens and name the different colors.	Talk about things you can ride in (e.g., cars, wagons, airplanes, buses).	Visit the zoo and look for tiny animals.	Name your neighbors and their pets.	Talk about the different types of furniture in a bedroom.	Sort the books in the house into two piles: big books and little books.
Name the appliances in the house (e.g., washer, dryer, stove, vacuum cleaner, refrigerator).	Look under furniture and talk about what you find.	Watch the clouds move across the sky. Talk about how they move.	Look outside and talk about the birds you see.	Talk about signs of danger (e.g., smoke coming from a house, sirens blaring).	Go for a bike ride and talk about bike safety.	Collect sticks outside and arrange them by length.
Visit a museum and talk about the exhibits.	Talk about things that help people stay dry (e.g., raincoat, galoshes, umbrella).	Help your child draw shapes on paper. Name each shape.	Look in a magazine or newspaper and draw circles around the numbers you find.	Talk about the "signs of spring."	Draw a family picture. Talk about who is tallest, shortest, oldest, and youngest.	Look back at this month's calendar, and talk about the important things that happened.

Talk! Talk! Talk!

May

Sunday	Monday	Tuesday	Wednesday	Thursday	Friday	Saturday
Look at this month's calendar and talk about the important dates. Draw a circle around those dates.	Visit the library and find books about vegetables. Talk about your favorite vegetables.	Go for a walk and count cars in people's driveways.	Make a map of your house and label each room.	Make a card for someone special.	Watch a cartoon and talk about what happened.	Go through a kitchen cupboard and sort the food by type (e.g., fruit, vegetables, pasta, snacks, cereal).
Read a story and have your child turn the pages.	Sort the laundry. Talk about light colors and dark colors.	Make cookies and talk about the colors of the different ingredients.	Talk about the things in the kitchen that are shaped like a square.	Eat pizza and talk about the different shapes on the pizza (e.g., round pepperoni, triangle or square slices).	Take a walk and talk about the plants you see.	Go to the store and buy vegetables. Talk about their colors.
Sing a favorite song. Make up actions to go with the words.	Form play dough or clay into shapes (e.g., balls, cones, boxes).	Talk about things that make people feel sad.	Go for a "listening walk" and talk about the different sounds you hear.	Find several boxes and sort them by size.	Find bugs outside and talk about what they look like.	Have another child over for a picnic lunch.
Talk about what you did yesterday.	Taste sugar and salt. Talk about foods that are sweet and foods that are salty.	Look through a jewelry box and describe the various items with words like *shiny, dull, old,* and *bright.*	Fill a jar with beans and use it as a shaker. Play music while shaking the shaker.	Make chocolate milk using milk and chocolate syrup. Talk about each step.	Talk about the weather and draw a picture of a rainy day.	Pick some flowers and weeds. Arrange the bouquet in a vase.
Plant a flower outside. Talk about how to care for the flower.	Go outside and look at the trees. Talk about the buds or leaves you see.	Measure your height and your child's. Talk about the difference.	Go for a walk and count all the trucks you see.	Hop over the lines in the sidewalk while counting each one.	Talk about the people who work in a hospital (e.g., doctors, nurses, assistants, custodians).	Look back at this month's calendar and talk about the important things that happened.

Talk! Talk! Talk!

June

Sunday	Monday	Tuesday	Wednesday	Thursday	Friday	Saturday
Look at this month's calendar and talk about the important dates. Draw a circle around those dates.	Pull weeds from the garden and talk about how they're different from the plants.	Go for a walk and talk about the colors of cars on the street.	Dig a small hole in the yard and pour water into it. Talk about what happens.	Sort socks into pairs and describe the different patterns and colors.	Play Follow the Leader while walking through the house.	Go barefoot outside to feel grass, mud, cement, and/or sand under your feet.
Put shoes on your hands and move forward and backward on your hands and feet.	Put money into a vending machine to buy a beverage.	Look for bugs under logs or rocks. Describe the bugs.	Chew bubble gum and blow bubbles. Talk about the sticky, pink gum and bubbles.	Draw a puppet face on your hand and make it talk.	Drop cotton balls and marbles into a bucket. Talk about the sounds you hear.	Play jump rope and sing a song or do a chant as you jump.
Read a book about a garden.	Shop for apples at the store. Compare red and green apples.	Listen to birds singing. Try to find birds of various colors.	Eat a picnic lunch in the yard or at the park. Play games after eating.	Take a walk and look for the tallest tree and the shortest tree you can find.	Bring in the mail from the mailbox and sort the various items by size.	Pick up small items with a kitchen tongs or tweezers. Drop the items into a bag.
Dust some furniture and talk about before and after.	Vacuum the carpet. Talk about loud and quiet sounds.	Count the number of pillows in the house and talk about their thicknesses.	Set the table. Talk about forks, knives, plates, and bowls.	Use spoons and pots to drum. Copy each other's simple patterns.	Take turns making different animal sounds.	Talk about different baby animals (e.g., kittens, puppies, cubs, calves, chicks).
Talk about different items that might be in people's backyards.	Visit a playground. Talk about different actions (e.g., digging, swinging, sliding, jumping, running).	Wriggle along on the floor like a snake and make a hissing sound.	Comb or brush the dolls and stuffed animals.	Talk about different types of emergencies (e.g., a fire in the house, someone choking, getting cut).	Go for a car ride. Look for schools, churches, and stores.	Look back at this month's calendar, and talk about the important things that happened.

Talk! Talk! Talk!

July

Sunday	Monday	Tuesday	Wednesday	Thursday	Friday	Saturday
Look at this month's calendar, and talk about the important dates. Draw a circle around those dates.	Take a walk and talk about things that grow (e.g., grass, flowers, trees).	Look for flags in the neighborhood. Talk about what different flags mean.	Make popsicles and talk about things that are frozen.	Water flowers in the yard or plants in the house. Talk about how water helps plants grow.	Put up a tent in the backyard and pretend to be camping.	Wash your feet with the garden hose. Talk about how the water feels.
Make shadows with your body. Stretch out your arms, and then scrunch into a ball.	Buy oranges at the store. Talk about the color, shape, and taste of an orange.	Run in place. Change your speed as you run.	Drink a beverage with a straw. Talk about how straws work.	Climb over and under chairs as you describe your movements.	Make Jell-O and talk about the texture before and after it has been chilled.	Put a rock in the sun and leave it for a while. Feel how hot it gets.
Wiggle your nose, fingers, and toes one at a time and then all together.	Listen for the wind. Talk about how the leaves sound when they move.	Blow across the top of a bottle and hear the whistle. Try various bottles.	Play in a sprinkler or hose. Run around, under, and through the spray.	Talk about different pets in the neighborhood.	Name three fun things to do in hot weather.	Give sets of directions to your child to follow (e.g., sit in a chair, touch your nose, wave).
Taste salty foods and describe the taste.	Go for a walk and talk about things you see on the ground.	Make a car or a house from a cardboard box. Draw identifying features on the box (e.g., a door, windows).	Find things in the cupboard that have blue labels.	Look at and talk about different types of shoes (e.g., sandals, slippers, tennis shoes).	Read a story about the rain. Talk about how rain can sound.	Count all the stairs in the house.
Look at the shadows from the trees in the morning and in the evening. Talk about how they switch direction.	Think of words that rhyme with buy.	Make fun hairstyles in your child's hair when it is soaped up during bathtime.	Talk and sing into a blowing fan. Talk about how your voice sounds.	Talk about clothes you would not wear in the summer (e.g., mittens, scarves, snow boots).	Make chalk drawings on the sidewalk or driveway. Label the drawings.	Look back at this month's calendar, and talk about the important things that happened.

Talk! Talk! Talk!

August

Sunday	Monday	Tuesday	Wednesday	Thursday	Friday	Saturday
Look at this month's calendar, and talk about the important dates. Draw a circle around the numbers.	Go for a walk and describe the houses you see using words like *tall*, *wide*, *square*, and *new*.	Move fast and slow while making shadows.	Find rough and smooth things in a kitchen drawer.	Have watermelon for a snack. Count the seeds you find.	Tiptoe quietly across a room. Then stomp loudly across a room.	Find things in the yard that are round. Talk about which items roll.
Buy bananas at the store. Talk about their color and shape. Use the bananas to make a snack.	Practice hitting a softball with a bat. Count the number of hits.	Shop for groceries. Name all the vegetables you see in the store.	Color a picture on a paper plate. Hang the picture on a kitchen cupboard.	Try on the different hats in the house. Talk about how each hat looks and feels.	Find the widest tree in the yard or the neighborhood. Then look for narrow trees.	Kick a big ball around the yard. Talk about how the ball moves.
Count all the windows in the house. Talk about open versus closed windows.	Use streamers, stickers, and balloons to decorate a bike or a wagon.	Cut out different shapes from colored paper and make a collage.	Read a story about flowers.	Press flowers in a book. Let them dry, then use them to create a picture.	Pick up objects in the yard and decide which are heavy and which are light.	Hold ribbons out in the wind and watch them move.
Look outside for machines that are used in construction.	Tape a leaf to paper and color around it. Remove the leaf and see the outline.	Spread jam on bread for a snack. Talk about how jam is made.	Pick up objects with your toes. Talk about how toes are different from fingers.	Wash a bicycle. Talk about the different parts of the bicycle.	Talk about words that rhyme with *hot*.	Take turns describing stuffed animals found around the house.
Make funny faces in a mirror. Then draw pictures of funny faces.	Dance and sing along to music.	String paper clips together to make a necklace. Count the paper clips.	Talk about all the things needed for a camping trip.	Find different containers in the house (e.g., a jar, an egg carton, a box, a bottle) and talk about their shapes.	Walk around the house or neighborhood looking for pink flowers. Draw a picture of your favorite flower.	Look back at this month's calendar, and talk about the important things that happened.

September

Sunday	Monday	Tuesday	Wednesday	Thursday	Friday	Saturday
Look at this month's calendar, and talk about the important dates. Draw a circle around those dates.	Do exercises and talk about the different movements you use.	Find light green and dark green plants and trees in the house and yard.	Talk about the names of the stuffed animals in the house.	Talk about and practice a fire escape route in your house.	Use paint to paint a rainbow. Label the different colors.	Make cookies with faces on them. Talk about facial parts.
Make a kite from paper and attach it to a string. Hold it out in the wind and talk about how it moves.	Learn a poem and recite it with actions.	Talk about tiny things you find in the house.	Look through photo albums and talk about what's happening in the various pictures.	Walk to a busy street and listen for traffic noises. Talk about being safe when near traffic.	Talk about the different shapes of clouds in the sky.	Make toast for breakfast. Cut the toast into different shapes (e.g., triangles, squares).
Read a favorite story. Have your child help tell parts of the story.	Go on a walk. Move fast and then move slowly.	Count the tables in the house. Find the biggest table and the smallest table.	Have a picnic in the park or in the backyard. Talk about the difference between *inside* and *outside*.	Tap wooden, plastic, and metal spoons against a tin can. Talk about the different sounds.	Play catch with a small ball. Throw the ball high and roll it low.	Build a tower from empty boxes. Talk about big and small boxes.
Make lemonade or Kool-Aid. Talk about each step.	Collect several bugs and put them in a jar with grass, sticks, and leaves. Describe each bug.	Toss wadded up socks into a laundry basket. Count the number of times the socks go in.	Help your child make a phone call to invite a friend over to play.	Cut a shape on the bottom half of a potato, dip it into food coloring, and press it onto paper to make potato prints.	Have your child look through a grocery ad and cut out favorite foods. Glue the pictures onto a paper plate.	Count to 5 or 10 using fingers or toes.
Help your child send a postcard to a relative.	Talk about at least two things you did yesterday.	Walk down the stairs, then crawl up the stairs.	Listen to music and do a funny dance.	Talk about all the things needed to wrap a present. Wrap a box in newspaper.	Look for pictures of horses in storybooks.	Look back at this month's calendar, and talk about the important things that happened.

Talk! Talk! Talk!

October

Sunday	Monday	Tuesday	Wednesday	Thursday	Friday	Saturday
Look at this month's calendar, and talk about the important dates. Draw a circle around those dates.	Talk about today's weather. Talk about yesterday's weather.	Clean out the toy box. Sort the toys.	Touch and name three body parts that come in pairs.	Wash dolls and toy cars in the bathtub. Talk about which are wet and which are dry.	Make different letter shapes with your body by bending and stretching.	Go outside and count all the things you can find that grow.
Walk around outside, and look for leaves on the ground. Try to make a big pile of leaves and a little pile of leaves.	Find soft things in the house. Talk about why they're soft.	Go outside and find a stick that is crooked and a stick that is straight.	Yawn really big. Talk about feeling sleepy.	Find orange things in the house.	Lie on your back, and move your legs like you're riding a bicycle. Move fast and then slow.	Name animals that live on a farm.
Talk about clothes people might wear in the fall (e.g., a sweater, pants, a jacket).	Look for things in the kitchen that are empty and things that are full.	Build tall and short towers with toy blocks.	Make a picture by gluing leaves onto a piece of paper.	Read a book about fall. Talk about what happens in the fall.	Make cookies shaped like triangles and circles.	Use paper towels or fabric strips to make clothes for small dolls.
Line up several chairs to make a pretend bus.	Fill a squirt bottle with water and spray it on the sidewalk outside. Watch if the water dries fast or slow.	Stack books and talk about thick books and thin books.	Find Halloween on the calendar. Count the number of days until Halloween.	Make a mask out of a paper bag. Draw a picture of the mask.	Decorate a shoebox to use as a house or a bed for a doll or a stuffed animal.	Look for squirrels outside. Count how many you find.
Talk about different Halloween costumes.	Read a Halloween story and have your child tell about his or her favorite part.	Carve a pumpkin to make a jack-o'-lantern.	Bake some pumpkin seeds and eat them.	Go outside at night and look at the stars in the sky. Talk about if there are many stars or just a few.	Sort different candies based on size, shape, or color.	Look back at this month's calendar, and talk about the important things that happened.

Talk! Talk! Talk!

November

Sunday	Monday	Tuesday	Wednesday	Thursday	Friday	Saturday
Look at this month's calendar and talk about the important dates. Draw a circle around those dates.	Read a story about friendship. Talk about friends.	Talk about things that are cold.	Take turns hiding and finding a small object. Hide it in, on, and under bigger objects.	Line up cans by height from tallest to shortest.	Talk about animals that made good house pets.	Turn on the lights in the house, then turn off every light. Talk about *on* and *off*.
Name clothes people wear to stay warm (e.g., a sweater, a coat, gloves, boots).	Talk about loud noises and quiet noises.	Count the toy cars and dolls in a toy box. Lay them out in a line to make a pattern (e.g., doll, car, doll, car).	Take a walk. Walk in front of, behind, and then beside each other.	Talk about arms. Find arms on bodies and arms on furniture.	Name things that can be opened (e.g., a door, an envelope, a box of cookies).	Look at items in a kitchen drawer and talk about their uses.
Put an object in a box. Shake the box and have your child guess what's inside.	Find a chair with short legs and a chair with long legs.	Trace an outline of your hand. Talk about what fingers can do.	Put objects above, below, and through other objects.	Put groceries away. Talk about the items and where they go.	Sort a box or bag of colorful candies into piles based on colors.	Find things that are scratchy and things that are furry.
Sort playing cards based on their color.	Float marshmallows in hot chocolate and watch them melt.	Wear all blue clothes and look for blue items in the house.	Look at the pictures in a favorite book and tell the story.	Close your eyes and smell different foods. Try to guess foods based on their scents.	Glue cotton balls onto paper to make a snow scene. Talk about how snow feels.	Talk about the body parts we use for smelling, the parts we use for seeing, and those we use for feeling.
Talk about objects that go together, (e.g., shoes and socks, salt and pepper, a fork and a spoon, a brush and a comb).	Go outside and count all the trees you see.	Talk about animals that can live in a person's house and animals that live in the forest.	Blow a piece of tissue across the table and talk about how it moves.	Perform a finger play or song about winter.	Talk about names of different relatives (e.g., *aunt, uncle, cousin*).	Look back at this month's calendar, and talk about the important things that happened.

Talk! Talk! Talk!

December

Sunday	Monday	Tuesday	Wednesday	Thursday	Friday	Saturday
Look at this month's calendar and talk about the important dates. Draw a circle around those dates.	Cut a snowflake out of folded white paper. Attach a string and hang the snowflake from the ceiling or a window.	Put pennies in a jar and rice in another jar. Shake the jars one at a time and compare their sounds.	Draw a face and talk about the different parts (e.g., eyelashes, forehead, nose, chin, dimples, ears).	Open both ends of a can. Talk through the can. Talk about how your voice sounds.	Blow puffs of air against a mirror. Talk about what you see.	Sort a pile of buttons by size or color.
Make a card to give to a special friend or relative.	Talk about items that need to be stored in the freezer.	Read a book about a snow person. Then draw a snow person.	Sing a song about winter. Make up actions to go with the song.	Go for an evening drive and look at stars or twinkling lights.	Count the buttons on a coat or sweater. Practice buttoning the buttons.	Make and display a special holiday decoration.
Wrap a present. Talk about the design on the wrapping paper.	Look in the refrigerator and find foods that are white.	Cut out footprint outlines and place them in a path around the house. Follow the footprints.	Watch a piece of ice melt. Talk about if it melts fast or slow.	Talk about all the white things in a room.	Using paper strips and tape, make paper chains. String the chains along a wall.	Draw pictures on a large sheet of paper and use the paper for wrapping a gift.
Go shopping to buy a present for a special person. Talk about what the person might like.	Bake cookies together. Talk about wet versus dry ingredients.	Talk about different feelings (e.g., excited, tired, happy, sad).	Talk about how things feel to the touch (e.g., soft, cold, fuzzy).	Make a decoration using ribbons and bows. Talk about the different colors.	Pick up a room in the house. Talk about where the different items belong and why.	Throw dry bread out to the birds and watch them eat it. Then draw a picture of a bird.
Play a following-directions game.	Move fast and then slow as you perform a variety of actions (e.g., waving, kicking, spinning).	Give every member of the family a hug and tell them you love them.	Roll play dough or clay into balls of different sizes. Talk about the sizes.	Look at the nighttime sky. Try to find the moon. Talk about its shape.	Draw a family picture and label each person by name.	Look back at this month's calendar, and talk about the important things that happened.

Talk! Talk! Talk!

References

AC Nielson Company. (1993). *The 1992–1993 report on television.* New York: Nielson Media Research.

American Academy of Pediatrics. (1995a). *Caring for your school-aged child: Ages 5 to 12.* New York: Bantam.

American Academy of Pediatrics Committee on Communications. (1995b). Children, adolescents, and television. *Pediatrics, 96*(Suppl. 4), 786–787.

Brown, R. (1973). A first language: The early stages. Cambridge, MA: Harvard University Press.

Bruner, J.S. (1978). Learning how to do things with words. In J.S. Bruner and R.A. Garton (Eds.), *Human growth and development* (pp. 62–84). Oxford, UK: Oxford University Press.

Butler, K. (1999). From oracy to literacy: Changing clinical perceptions. *Topics in Language Disorders, 20*(1), 14–32.

Cole, K. (1995). Curriculum models and language facilitation in the preschool years. In M. Fey and J. Reichle (Eds.), *Communication intervention for school-age children* (pp. 39–60). Baltimore: Brookes.

Dore, J. (1974). A pragmatic description of early language development. *Journal of Psycholinguistic Research, 3,* 343–350.

Duchan, J.F. (1984). Language assessment: The pragmatics revolution. In R.C. Naremore (Ed.), *Language science* (pp. 147–180). San Diego: College-Hill.

Fey, M.E. (1986). *Language intervention with young children.* San Diego, CA: College-Hill.

Fey, M.E., and Cleave, P.L. (1997). Two models of grammar facilitation in children with language impairments: Phase 2. *Journal of Speech, Language, and Hearing Research, 40,* 5–20.

Fey, M.E., Cleave, P.L., Long, S.H., and Hughes, D.L. (1993). Two approaches to the facilitation of grammar in language-impaired children: An experimental evaluation. *Journal of Speech and Hearing* Research, 36, 141–157.

Girolametto, L.E. (1986). *Developing dialogue skills of mothers and their developmentally delayed children: An intervention study.* Unpublished doctoral dissertation, University of Toronto, Ontario, Canada.

Girolametto, L.E., Greenberg, J., and Manolson, H.A. (1986). Developing dialogue skills: The Hanen early intervention program. *Seminars in Speech and Language, 7,* 367–382.

Hart, B., and Risley, T. (1995). *Meaningful differences in the everyday experience of young American children.* Baltimore: Brookes.

Hart, B., and Risley, T. (1999). The social world of children: Learning to talk. *The Clinical Connection, 12*(3), 7–10.

Muma, J.R. (1971). Language intervention: Ten techniques. *Language, Speech, and Hearing Services in Schools, 1*(5), 7–17.

Noonan, M., and McCormick, L. (1993). *Early intervention in natural environments: Methods and procedures.* Pacific Grove, CA: Brooks/Cole Publishing.

Norris, J.A., and Hoffman, P.R. (1990). Language intervention within naturalistic environments. *Language, Speech, and Hearing Services in Schools, 21,* 72–84.

Strasburger, V.C. (1993). Children, adolescents, and the media: Five crucial issues. *Adolescent Media: State of the Art Review, 4,* 479–493.

Tannock, R., Girolametto, L.E., and Siegel, L. (1992). The interactive model of language intervention: Evaluation of its effectiveness for pre-school-aged children with developmental delay. *American Journal of Mental Retardation, 97*(2), 145–160.

Watson, C. (1993). *Making Hanen happen.* Toronto, Canada: Hanen.